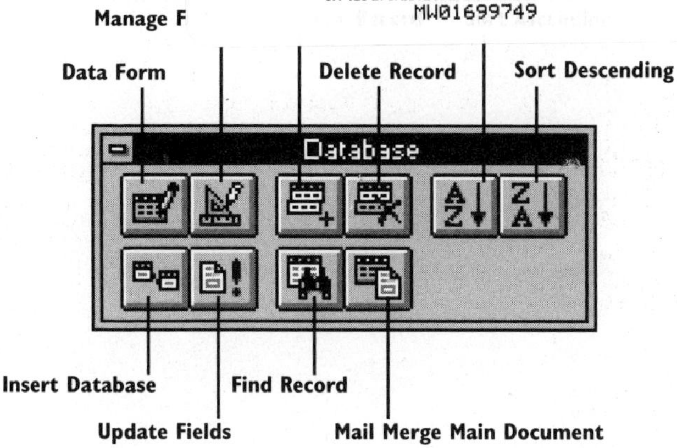

Header and Footer Toolbar

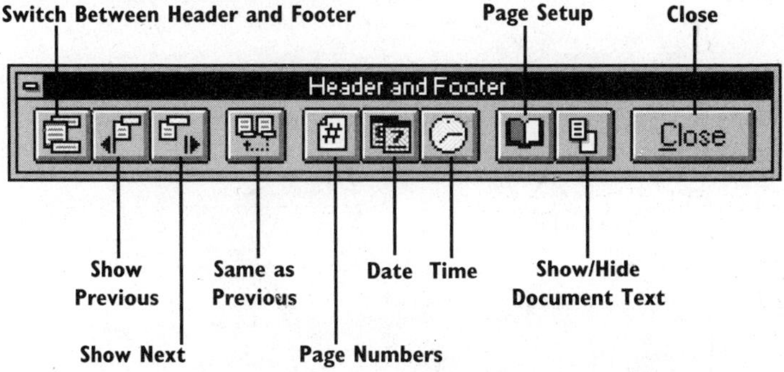

Word for Windows
Quick & Easy Reference

Word for Windows™

Quick & Easy Reference

Ron Mansfield

SYBEX®

San Francisco
Paris
Düsseldorf
Soest

Developmental Editor: Sarah Wadsworth
Editor and Typesetter: Guy Hart-Davis
Technical Editor: Bob Campbell
Proofreader/Production Coordinator: Janet K. Boone
Indexer: Liz Cunningham
Cover Designer: Archer Design
Cover Illustrator: Richard Miller

Screen reproductions produced with Collage Plus.

Collage Plus is a trademark of Inner Media Inc.

SYBEX is a registered trademark of SYBEX Inc.

TRADEMARKS: SYBEX has attempted throughout this book to distinguish proprietary trademarks from descriptive terms by following the capitalization style used by the manufacturer.

SYBEX is not affiliated with any manufacturer.

Library of Congress Card Number: 93-87028

ISBN: 0-7821-1380-X

Manufactured in the United States of America

10 9 8 7 6 5 4 3 2 1

ACKNOWLEDGMENTS

I would like to thank Sarah "The Enforcer" Wadsworth for strategic limitation and targeting; Guy "Text Butcher" Hart-Davis for judicious application of Occam's Razor; Bob "Sparks" Campbell for a violent but friendly technical edit; Janet "Rerag Queen" Boone for scrutinizing the proofs into pages; and Liz "Dex" Cunningham for nailing down everything that moved and quite a few things that didn't.

TABLE OF CONTENTS

INTRODUCTION

Word for Windows version 6 is a major upgrade to an already full-featured word-processing program, with many new features added and many old features improved. This book will help you come to grips with Word 6 quickly.

Who Needs This Book?

If you're upgrading from Word 2.0 for Windows, this book will ease the transition and provide information about Word 6's many new features. If you're upgrading from another word-processing application, this book will supply the information you need to complete everyday tasks (and some less frequent ones) with Word 6.

The *Word for Windows Quick & Easy Reference* is organized alphabetically to help you quickly find what you need. Complicated procedures are made simple in step-by-step lists, and the book is spiced with useful info and hints in nine different flavors—such as Note, Tip, Warning, Shortcut, and Techno Note—pinpointed with icons.

This book assumes a little knowledge of Word. If you are a new user, consider additional resources like my *Mastering Word 6 for Windows Special Edition* (also from SYBEX), a comprehensive, illustrated guide to everyday word-processing and desktop-publishing tasks that contains lots of background information, tips, and exercises not found here.

Book Conventions

We've used some standard conventions and typographer's tricks to make the book easier to read (and keep it concise and pocketable!). While most of them will be obvious, scan the next few paragraphs just in case.

Keyboard Notations

Here's how we've represented keyboard maneuvers:

- Whenever you need to hold down one key, then press another, you'll see the keys separated by + signs. For instance, Ctrl+S means hold down Ctrl and press S.
- **Boldface text** usually indicates things you are expected to type. Also, some keys (such as the arrow keys and the Enter key) are indicated by icons.
- The Enter key is represented as ↵. So, if you are being asked to type a filename and then press the Enter key in an example, you'll read something like "Type **readme.doc**, then press ↵."

Menu Commands

As a shortcut and an eyecatcher, we've used a special convention to indicate menu commands. When we want you to choose a menu command, it will follow this pattern: *menu name* ➤ *command*—for example, "choose Tools ➤ Options" means "pull down the Tools menu and choose Options."

The underlining indicates the *hot keys* for menus and commands. Pressing the hot key letter is a way of choosing the command. For example, if we say "Choose File ➤ Save," you could hit Alt to activate the menu bar and then press F and S instead of choosing Save from the File menu with the mouse.

Word for Windows

Command Reference

Annotations

Use either Hidden text or Word's Insert ➤ Annotations command to include author's notes in text.

Inserting Annotations

1. Place the insertion point where you want to insert the annotation, or select the item you wish to discuss.
2. Pick Insert ➤ Annotation (*not* View ➤ Annotations). You'll see the annotation window pane, and Word will insert initials (with any luck, yours—from the User Info tab of the Tools ➤ Options dialog box) as hidden text.
3. Type the note.
4. Either choose Close, or leave the pane visible as you work.

note

Select View ➤ Annotations to view annotations.

Editing and Protecting Annotations

1. Choose Tools ➤ Protect Document. The Protect Document dialog box will appear.
2. Choose the protection you desire (Annotations).
3. Enter a password and click OK.
4. Repeat it when Word asks. Click OK or press ↵.
5. Remember the password....

warning

Punctuation counts when entering passwords.

Incorporating Annotations

You can copy and paste text from the annotation pane into the document. Drag-and-drop works here too!

Printing Annotations

To print just the annotations, visit the Print dialog box (File ➤ Print or Ctrl+P) and choose Annotations from the Print What list.

To print a document and its annotations, choose Document in the Print dialog box's Print What list, then click the Options button to reveal the Print Tab. Choose Annotations from the options list.

Moving and Removing Annotations

Move and delete annotations by treating their annotation marks as you would any other character in a document.

AutoCorrect

The primary reason for AutoCorrect is to fix typos like *teh* when you meant to type *the*. Word will watch you type and change things for you. For instance, if you type **(r)** or **(R)**, Word will replace those characters with the Registered symbol (®).

To use Word's built-in AutoCorrect entries, you just type along as usual. Word will make changes when it thinks they are needed. You can see a list of the current auto corrections by scrolling in the AutoCorrect dialog box (reached with Tools ➤ AutoCorrect). In addition to correcting typos, you can use AutoCorrect to convert "shorthand" into longer text strings.

Creating Your Own AutoCorrect Entries

1. Open the AutoCorrect dialog box with Tools ➤ AutoCorrect.
2. Type the "name" (the text string you wish to replace) in the Replace box.
3. Type the replacement in the With box, then click Add.
4. Make any other entries or changes.
5. Click OK when done.

Editing AutoCorrect Entries

1. Correct and select the entry in a document.
2. Open the AutoCorrect dialog box (Tools ➤ AutoCorrect).
3. Type the old Replace name.
4. When the Replace button undims, click it.
5. Answer Yes to the *Do you want to redefine* question. The entry will be updated.

Deleting AutoCorrect Entries

1. Open the AutoCorrect dialog box (Tools ➤ AutoCorrect).

2. Select the victim.
3. Click the Delete button. The entry will be deleted.

AutoFormat

AutoFormat inspects your document and suggests formatting changes that you can accept or reject. Word can locate and reformat headings, change straight quotes to curly quotes, and more:

1. Open the document you wish to reformat.
2. Choose Format ➢ AutoFormat.
3. If you wish to change the way AutoFormat works, click the Options button. Uncheck the formatting tasks you don't want it to perform. For instance, if you don't want Word to preserve any styles you've already applied, uncheck the appropriate box.
4. When you have specified any necessary changes to Word's usual AutoFormatting habits, click OK to go back to the AutoFormat dialog box.
5. Click OK in the AutoFormat dialog box. Word will go to work.
6. To see and review each proposed change, choose Review Changes. To apply further formatting via the Style Gallery click the Style Gallery button; or simply accept or reject all changes.

AutoText

AutoText is the replacement for Word's old Glossary command. It's an easy way to store and retrieve "boilerplate" text, graphics, addresses, letter closings, memo distribution lists, tables, logos, and just about anything else that you can create with Word. You can store AutoText entries with the NORMAL template so that they are always available, or with other templates for specialty projects.

Creating AutoText Entries

Select whatever it is you wish to memorialize, then choose Edit ➤ AutoText and click Add.

techno note

To store the paragraph formatting with the entry, include paragraph marks in your selection(Even if you store an entry *with* paragraph formatting, you can later insert it *without* formatting if you wish.)

shortcut

Click the AutoText button (a keyboard with a finger pointing at it) on the Standard toolbar to open the AutoText dialog box.

Saving AutoText Entries

1. Before saving an entry, you are given a chance to review and change the automatic entry name Word assigns. To change the name, just type a new one in the name box. Names can be up to 32 characters long, and spaces are permitted.
2. If you want an entry to be available whenever you use Word, leave the default choice, All Documents

(Normal.dot), in the drop-down Make AutoText Entry Available To list. To attach an entry to a different template, pick one from the list.

3. Click the Add button.

Using AutoText Entries

Once you've saved some AutoText entries, you can insert them using several different techniques. Place the insertion point where you want the entry to be inserted.

- Type all or part of an AutoText entry's name, then click the AutoText toolbar button.
- Type all or part of an AutoText entry's name, then press F3.
- Type all or part of an AutoText entry's name, then press Alt+Ctrl+V.
- Choose Edit ➤ AutoText (you'll see a preview), then pick an entry from the scrolling name list by either double-clicking or clicking once and then clicking the Insert button or pressing ↵.

Word will insert the entry. Edit it as you would any other text or graphic or other document element.

Editing AutoText Entries

1. Insert the entry in a document.
2. Edit and reformat it as necessary.
3. Select the corrected entry and any necessary punctuation, paragraph marks, spaces following, etc.
4. Visit the AutoText dialog box (Edit ➤ AutoText).

5. Rename the entry, if necessary.
6. Click the Add button.
7. Answer Yes to the *Do you want to redefine* question.

Deleting AutoText Entries

1. Open the AutoText dialog box (Edit ➤ AutoText).
2. Select the doomed item from the scrolling list.
3. Look in the Preview box or insert the entry and check to be *certain* that this is the entry you wish to delete.
4. Click Delete.

Bookmarks

You can insert invisible electronic bookmarks in your Word documents to help you move between and refer to particular items. To use bookmarks, you simply define things of interest as bookmarks and visit or refer to them as necessary.

Inserting a Bookmark

1. Either move the insertion point to the item of interest, or select the item.
2. Choose Edit ➤ Bookmark (Ctrl+Shift+F5). You'll see the Bookmark dialog box.
3. Give the bookmark a unique name consisting of up to 40 characters. Spaces are *not* allowed, so use an underscore instead.

4. Click Add. (If the button is dimmed, check to see that the name is less than 40 characters long and contains no spaces). Word will add the bookmark and close the dialog box.

Going to a Bookmark

Once you've defined some bookmarks, you can go to them in one of two ways. If you select Edit ➤ Go To and click Bookmark in the Go to What box, you'll see a drop-down list of bookmarks. Double-click on a bookmark's name to go there. Alternatively, click the Go To button in the Bookmark dialog box; Word will go to the selected bookmark without displaying the Go To dialog box.

tip

In the Bookmark dialog box, you can sort the list either by name or by the location of the bookmark in the document.

Deleting Bookmarks

1. Visit the Bookmark dialog box (Edit ➤ Bookmark).
2. Choose the desired bookmark name.
3. Click the Delete button.
4. Click Close. The bookmark disappears and the previously marked items remain.

To delete a bookmark *and* the items it marks:

1. Turn on Bookmark markers in the View tab of the Options dialog box (Tools ➤ Options).
2. Select the item and both bookmark markers.

3. Delete as usual (Cut, press Delete, etc.). The mark and the items(s) will disappear.

Borders and Shading

You can apply various border treatments and shading to single paragraphs or groups of paragraphs.

Creating Lines with Format ➤ Borders and Shading

You can use Format ➤ Borders and Shading to create lines as well as boxes. You adjust the horizontal *length* of borders or lines by adjusting a paragraph's width with indent markers or the Paragraph dialog box.

1. Place the insertion point in the paragraph of interest, or select elements to be formatted—multiple paragraphs, graphics, etc.
2. Adjust indents if necessary to define the desired width for the borders.
3. Reveal the Borders toolbar (use the Border button or View ➤ Toolbars).
4. With the Borders toolbar open, choose the desired line thickness from its drop-down list.
5. Click on the button corresponding to the desired border (No Border, Outside, Inside, Right, Left, Bottom, or Top).
6. Pick shading if you like from the drop-down shading list. Watch your document change as you work.

Creating Custom Borders and Lines

1. Place the insertion point in the paragraph of interest, or select elements to be formatted—multiple paragraphs, graphics, etc.
2. Open the Borders and Shading dialog box (Format ➤ Borders and Shading).
3. Click on the appropriate border guides in the sample to turn them on or off.
4. Click on the line type(s) you wish. Watch the Border Sample part of the Borders and Shading dialog box as you work. Click OK when you're done.

Increasing the Space between Borders and Text

To add extra space between the text contained within borders and the borders themselves, specify a measurement (in points) in the From Text portion of the Borders tab of the Borders and Shading dialog box.

Controlling Border Width

To change border width, select the paragraph(s) containing the border formatting and change the paragraph's indents.

Adding and Changing Shading

You can use either the Borders toolbar or the Borders and Shading dialog box to add and change shading. The smaller the percentage, the lighter the shading—100% is solid black.

1. Place the insertion point in the paragraph of interest, or select elements to be shaded—multiple paragraphs, graphics, etc.
2. Open the Borders and Shading dialog box with Format ➤ Borders and Shading.
3. Click on the Shading tab.
4. Scroll through the Shading list and select a percentage. You will see the effect in the Preview box.
5. Click OK when you're satisfied.
6. Be sure to test print new designs.

Removing Borders and Shading

1. Select the objects with the borders or shading you wish to remove.
2. Display the Borders toolbar (View ➤ Toolbars).
3. Click on the No Border button (the rightmost button).
4. If shading has been applied, choose Clear from the Shading list, or type **C** in place of the displayed percentage and press ↵.

Bullets

Word lets you apply various styles of bullets and numbering automatically to your documents. Here's how:

1. Select Format ➤Bullets and Numbering to open the Bullets and Numbering dialog box.
2. Make sure the Bulleted tab is foremost.
3. Select a style of bullets and click OK.

tip

To use different bullet characters, choose the Modify button in the Bullets and Numbering dialog box and make adjustments in the Modify Bulleted List dialog box

note

To use numbers rather than bullets, select the Numbered tab of the Bullets and Numbering dialog box and select a suitable format.

Captions

The Caption feature automatically numbers things, lets you label them, then renumbers them if you move them or otherwise change their sequence in a document. There are a variety of appearance options as well.

1. Select the item to be captioned.
2. Choose Insert ➤ Caption to open the Caption dialog box.
3. Word proposes a caption label which you can accept as-is or edit. For example, you can type descriptive text.
4. Change the default appearance options if you wish, by visiting the Position List and Numbering dialog box.
5. Click OK to insert the label. Be patient, it takes a moment.

To automatically add captions to items of a particular type (all drawings, for instance), use the AutoCaption dialog box, reached with the AutoCaption button in the Caption dialog box.

To automatically caption things:

1. Choose Insert ➤ Caption to open the Caption dialog box.
2. Click the AutoCaption button.
3. Pick a type of item to automatically caption. You can pick more than one type for the same caption label (For instance, you can pick Microsoft drawings and Word pictures.) Inserting either will have the same effect.
4. Pick a label type from the Use Label list or create your own with the New Label button.
5. Pick a position for the label (Above or Below the item).
6. Change the numbering scheme if you like.
7. Repeat steps 3 through 6 for each different type of caption you want.
8. Click OK.

To revise a caption, just edit it like any other text. To change all of the captions of a given type (*Figure* to *FIG*, for instance), select a caption in text, visit the Caption or AutoCaption dialog box and pick a different label from the Use Label List.

Changing Case

Word lets you change the case of text you've already typed in two ways: by using the Change Case dialog box or (more quickly) by using the Change Case toggle keys (Shift+F3). The Change Case dialog box gives you more options:

1. Select the text you wish to change.
2. Choose Format ➤ Change Case.

3. Choose the desired case option: Sentence Case (first letter of first word capitalized), lowercase, UPPERCASE, Title Case (first letter of all major words capitalized), or tOGGLE cASE.
4. Click OK.

When you change case using the Change Case dialog box, the characters themselves change to the specified case, just as if you had retyped them using the new capitalization scheme. Undo works here.

shortcut

If you simply want to switch between Sentence Case, Uppercase, and lowercase, select the text and press Shift+F3 to cycle through these options.

tip

To have your text appear as ALL CAPS but retain its actual capitalization, select Format ➤ Font and check the All Caps check box in the Font dialog box. Alternatively, press Ctrl+Shift+A.

tip

For SMALL CAPS like these, select Format ➤ Font and check the Small Caps check box in the Font dialog box. Alternatively, press Ctrl+Shift+K.

Columns

To quickly arrange your text into columns, click the Columns button on the Formatting toolbar and drag to select from one to six columns. When you release the mouse button, Word automatically determines the appropriate width of columns and the amount of white space between columns based on the page and document settings.

Creating Multiple-Column Designs

To create different columns (even on the same page) select the text to be "columnized" and specify column settings with the Columns button on the Formatting toolbar or the Columns dialog box. Word will apply the settings only to the selected text and insert necessary breaks automatically.

Drag columns to different widths using margin markers. Start by placing the insertion point in the desired column, change to Page Layout view if necessary, and display the rulers if they aren't already on screen. Click on the Margin Marker button in the ruler to display the margin markers, then drag any marker and the columns will adjust to their new width.

Adding Lines between Columns

To add decorative lines between columns, place the insertion point in a column that you wish to decorate. Then choose Format ➤ Columns and choose Line Between.

Forcing Column Breaks

Place the insertion point where you want the column break,

then choose Insert ➤ Break, specify Column, and click OK. Remove breaks by highlighting them and pressing Delete.

Evening Out Uneven Columns

Place the insertion point after the last character in the text and choose Insert ➤ Break. Choose Continuous in the Sections area, then click OK. The column bottoms will align.

Removing Columns Document-wide

Select all of the text (Edit ➤ Select All), then use the toolbar's Columns button to specify a single column.

Cross Referencing

Cross referencing lets you say things like *see Chapter 29 for details*, then have Word automatically update the reference if you change the chapter number. Cross references are not limited to chapter numbers—they can refer to just about anything, including headings, footnotes, endnotes, captions, etc.

Creating Cross References

1. Begin by typing the in-text reference followed by a quotation mark (**See"** for example).
2. Choose Insert ➤ Cross-reference. You'll see the Cross-reference dialog box.
3. Pick the Reference Type that will tie the in-text reference to the item you wish to reference (Figure, for instance).

4. Choose the item you wish to reference in the scrolling For Which list.
5. Click Insert. You'll see some new information at the insertion point. This is actually a field. (See *Fields* on page 26 to learn more about fields.)
6. Click Close or make other cross references first, then Close.

Once you've created cross references, they will be updated when you print or switch to Print Preview. To update them immediately at any time, select the entire document and press F9.

note

If you delete a cross-referenced item, Word will alert you.

Customizing Word

Word lets you change its standard menu settings, toolbars, and keyboard shortcuts.

Displaying Toolbars

Select View ➤ Toolbars and mark the check boxes for the toolbars you want to see.

tip

To quickly display a toolbar, right-click on a displayed toolbar and then click the name of the toolbar on the shortcut menu. To hide a displayed toolbar, repeat the process.

Changing Word's Predefined Toolbars

Display the toolbars you want to see. Select Tools ➤ Customize, select the Toolbars tab, select a category in the Categories box, and then drag the button or item to where you want it on the toolbar. To delete a button, drag it off the toolbar.

Moving a Toolbar Button

Hold down Alt and drag the button to where you want it. To copy a button, hold down Ctrl+Alt and drag the button to where you want it.

Assigning an Item to a Toolbar Button

Select Tools ➤ Customize, choose the Toolbars tab, select the right template, select the category containing the item to add, and drag the item name from the box to the right of the Categories box to the toolbar. Select a button, then click the Assign button.

Changing Word's Menus

Word gives you a lot of flexibility with its menus. You can add or delete menu items, rename menus, and even add menus of your own.

Adding a Menu Item

Select Tools ➤ Customize and click the Menus tab. Select the template in which the item is stored, select the category to which the item belongs, and select the item you want to assign. Then choose the menu you want, choose a position for the new item, choose a name for the item, and click the Add or Add Below button.

Removing a Menu Item

Press Ctrl+Alt+– and click the menu item you want to remove.

Adding a New Menu

Select Tools ➤ Customize, choose the Menus tab, and select the template for the new menu. Then select the Menu Bar button, enter the name for the menu (use an ampersand [&] before a letter to designate a hot key), position the menu, and click the Add or Add After button.

Changing Keyboard Shortcuts

Select Tools ➤ Customize and select the Keyboard tab. Then select the category containing the item you want, select the command, enter the new keyboard shortcut, and click the Assign button.

Date and Time Entries

You can easily insert dates and times in your documents:

1. Position the insertion point.
2. Choose Insert ➤ Date and Time.
3. Pick the desired format from the scrolling list.
    - If the Insert as Field check box is checked, Word will update the date and time entry whenever you print the document.
4. Click OK.

note

The Header and Footer pane also contains buttons for inserting times and dates. See *Headers and Footers* on page 44.

Drawing

Place the insertion point where you want the drawing to appear and click the Draw button on the Standard toolbar. The Drawing toolbar will appear, and you can use its many features to create a drawing right in your document. Visit on-line help while drawing to learn more about the drawing tools.

Drop Caps

A drop cap is a large initial capital letter at the start of a paragraph, usually set into the text.

1. Format the body text the way you like it. Be sure you are happy with things like margins, fonts, and so on. Single-space the text.
2. Select the character or characters you want to drop, and choose Format ➤ Drop Cap. You'll see the Drop Cap dialog box.
3. If you want to use a different font for the drop cap, choose it from the drop-down Font menu.
4. Choose Dropped Position for traditional-looking drop caps or choose In Margin to place drop caps in the margin.

5. The Lines to Drop box proposes the number of lines the cap will drop. Pick the desired number of lines from the drop-down line list.
6. When you click OK, Word places the specified text in a frame and positions the frame for you.
    - If you are not in Page Layout view, Word will prompt you to switch to it.
7. Use the character, frame, and paragraph tools to modify Word's settings for the drop cap.

Envelopes and Labels

Word can print addresses on envelopes by looking for the addresses in your documents (the inside address of a letter, for instance), or you can type an address in the Envelopes and Labels dialog box. To reach the Envelopes and Labels dialog box, select Tools ➤ Envelopes and Labels. The dialog box lets you:

- Print envelopes containing one-time addresses that you type into the dialog box itself.
- Copy an address from your document for envelope printing.
- Type envelope addresses, then insert them into your letters or other Word documents.

Setting Up a Return Address

1. If you have more than one printer, choose the one to use.
2. Open the Envelopes and Labels dialog box by choosing Tools ➤ Envelopes and Labels.
3. Click on the Envelope tab if it is not foremost.

4. If Word finds an address in the current open Word document, you will see it in the Delivery Address portion of the dialog box.
5. Type your return address in the large box labeled Return Address. (Part of the address may be already filled out automatically, based on your Word User Info.)
6. When you are happy with the spelling and appearance of your return address, try test-printing on a plain #10 ($4^{1}/_{8}$ × $9\frac{1}{2}$") envelope. Word assumes that you can center-feed envelopes in your printer. If you can't, click on the envelope in the Feed section of the dialog box to bring up the Printing Options tab of the Envelope Options dialog box.
7. Select a combination that will work with your printer, then click OK.
8. Place an envelope in your printer.
9. Back in the Envelopes tab of the Envelopes and Labels dialog box, click Print to ensure that envelopes will print properly.

Suppressing Return Addresses

If you always plan to use envelopes that contain preprinted return addresses, you can make sure that nothing prints by making the Return Address area blank. Or you can have a return address typed there, and suppress its printing by checking the Omit box.

Printing Envelopes with New Addresses

You can either type an envelope address directly into the Envelopes and Labels dialog box, or select an address in your letter or other Word document, then open the Envelopes and Labels dialog box.

Adding an Envelope Page to Documents

Clicking on the Add to Document button in the Envelopes and Labels dialog box adds an envelope page to the beginning of your document. Word takes care of all the details. You can see what it does by switching to Print Preview with two pages showing.

Changing Addresses

Once you've inserted an envelope page in your document, you can change the envelope and inside address at any time.

Specifying Envelope Sizes, Fonts, and Other Options

Word lets you specify envelope sizes (both standard and custom), fonts used for delivery, return addresses, and more. Selected the options on the two tabs in the Envelope Options dialog box.

Adding Bar Codes to Speed Postal Delivery

If you are planning to send mail within the United States, you can ask Word to print bar codes on your envelopes. These will speed automated mail sorting. Word provides two coding techniques—POSTNET for regular mail and FIM-A for "courtesy reply" mail. Check the box or boxes you desire.

Feeding Envelopes

The Printing Options tab in the Envelope Options dialog box is where you tell Word how you plan to feed envelopes. The choices vary with the chosen printer. If you have multiple trays, you specify the tray containing envelopes (upper, lower, etc.). Click Reset to return to the default settings for the chosen printer.

Printing Labels

Label printing is a lot like envelope printing, except you have even more options. For instance, you can print single labels or sheets of labels. Word knows the dimensions for many different industry-standard stocks from Avery and others.

Including Graphics on Envelopes

1. Select Tools ➤ Envelopes and Labels and make sure the Envelope tab is selected in the Envelopes and Labels dialog box.
2. Click on either the Add To Document or Change Document button.
3. Switch to Page Layout if you're not already in it.
4. Paste or create a graphic and frame it (using Insert ➤ Frame), then move it into position as you would any other framed item.
5. Make any other changes that you like (rearrange or reformat lines of text in the inside address, for instance).

At this point, the envelope is one of a kind and in a separate section at the top of your current document. You can either save the document and print the envelope along with the rest of the document, or save the document as a template for repeated use. If you want the artwork to appear on *all* of your envelopes, you can select the art and create a special AutoText entry called EnvelopeExtra 1 or EnvelopeExtra 2.

Exiting Word

To quit Word, choose File ➤ Exit. If you have any unsaved changes, Word will ask if you want to save them before exiting.

shortcut

Hit Alt+F4 to exit Word or most Windows applications.

Fields

Fields are special codes you use to tell Word to insert information in your documents. You can insert codes to add and automatically update text, graphics, and so on.

Inserting a Field

Select Insert ➤ Field, select the category of field you want, and select the field you want. Choose the Options button to add switches or formatting to the field you selected, then select OK.

Displaying Field Codes and Results

Place the insertion point in the field, click the right mouse button to display the pop-up shortcut menu, and choose Toggle Field Codes; or select Tools ➤ Options, choose the View tab, and check the Field Codes check box.

To view field codes and results simultaneously, split the document window into panes and set different view options for each pane.

To display field results shaded, select Tools ➤ Options, choose the View tab, pull down the Field Shading list, and choose Always.

Formatting Fields

Format either the field result itself or the field code just as you would any other Word text.

Changing the Contents of Fields

Put the insertion point in the field, display the field codes by pressing Shift+F9, edit the field, and then display the field result again by pressing Shift+F9.

Updating Fields

To Update	Do This
a single field	right-click in the field and choose Update from the shortcut menu.
all fields in a document	choose Edit➤ Select All, right-click, and choose Update Field from the shortcut menu.
fields when you print	select Tools ➤ Options, select the Print tab, and check the Update Fields check box.

Locking and Unlocking Fields

To lock a field, place the cursor in the field and press Ctrl+F11 or Ctrl+3.

To unlock a field so it can once again be updated, place the cursor in the field and press Ctrl+Shift+F11.

To unlink a field so it can never again be updated, place the cursor in the field and press Ctrl+Shift+F9 or Ctrl+6.

Moving from Field to Field

To move between fields, select Edit ➤ Goto, select Field in the Go to What box, and enter the name of the field (or accept Any Field). Choose the Next button to find the next occurrence of the chosen field or the Previous button to find the previous occurrence.

shortcut

Press F11 to go to the next field or Shift+F11 to go to the previous field.

Find

Word's Find feature helps you quickly locate text, formats, special characters, and combinations thereof. You need not limit your searches to text. You can look for section marks, graphics, paragraph marks, and more. When using the Find command (as opposed to Replace), Word finds what you've requested, then scrolls to the found item and its surrounding text without modifying anything.

You must click in the document window to work with the found item. You can leave the Find dialog box out on your screen as you work, flipping between it and your document window.

To do a search:

1. Choose Edit ➤ Find.
2. Specify text and special characters (if any) to find.
3. Specify formatting characteristics (if any) to find.
4. Tell Word where to search and in which direction.
5. Use the Special menu to search for things like section breaks, paragraph marks, styles, etc.
6. Check off any special search requests like Match Case or Find Whole Words Only.
7. Click Find Next to start the search.
8. When Word finds what you want, return to the document.
9. To find again, click the Find Next button in the dialog box.

Finding Text

Choose Edit ➤ Find or press Ctrl+F to display the Find dialog box. Move to the text area of the Find What box and type enough text (a maximum of 255 characters) for an accurate, unambiguous search, then click the Find Next button.

Finding Special Characters

The Special drop-down list is a convenient way to enter certain special characters like tab marks, nonbreaking spaces, etc., when constructing a search request. Place the insertion point in the Find What box where you want the special character to go, and choose the desired character from the drop-down list.

Performing Advanced Searches

To perform advanced searches for combinations of things (such as both *bet* and *bat*), you use things called *operators*. They will remind you of wildcards, if you know what those are. For instance, to find either *bet* or *bat*, you would place **b?t** in your Find What box and check Use Pattern Matching. If you forget to check Use Pattern Matching, the results will not be what you expect.

Here's the list of operators you can use with Word and what they help you do:

Operator	Lets You Find
?	A single character: **b?t** finds *bat*, *bet*, *bit*, and *bat*
*	Any string of characters: **b*d** finds *bed*, *befuddled*, and *blood*
[characters]	Any of the characters in parens: **b[eo]d** finds *bed* and *bod* but not *bid*
[character-character]	Any character in the range: **b[a-i]d** finds *bed* and *bid* but not *bod*
[!character]	Any single character except the one in parens: **b[!i]d** finds *bed* and *bod* but not *bid*
[!Range of characters]	Any single character *except* those in the specified range
character{n}	Any n occurrences of the preceding character: **ble{2}d** finds *bleed* but not *bled*
character{n,}	At least n occurrences of the preceding character: **b{1,}** finds *bled* and *bleed*
character{n,m}	The specified range of characters: **10{2,3}** finds *100* and *1000* but not *10*

Operator	Lets You Find
character@	One or more occurrences of the preceding character: **ble@d** finds *bled* and *bleed*
<text	The beginning of a word: **<man** finds *manhole* and *manage*
text>	The end of a word. **in>** finds *in* and *herein* but not *interfere*

techno note

To search for characters used as operators ({, ! *, etc.), separate them with a backslash. For instance, to find the asterisk, search for *****.

Find File

Word's Find File feature (reached by choosing File ➤ Find File) is a powerful tool that helps you locate, list, sort, examine, open, and print documents based on simple or complex search criteria.

1. Choose File ➤ Find File to open the Find File dialog box.
2. Specify the location (drive C:, for instance) by choosing it from the drop-down Location list.
3. Tell Word to search subdirectories by checking the Include subdirectories box.
4. Type the filename search criteria in the File Name box.
5. Click the OK button (if it is dimmed, you probably haven't specified a location) or press ↵. In a moment you'll see a list of potential matches.
6. To examine a found file closely, click on its name.

Using the View Drop-Down Menu

The View drop-down menu lets you see (preview) the contents of the file or review its statistics (creator, last saved, size, and such). The window then displays available info. If you've entered summary information, you can read that here as well.

Using the Buttons in the Find File Dialog Box

Clicking the Open button at the bottom of the Find File dialog box will open the document as usual. Clicking Search will take you back to the Search dialog box. Print opens the document and presents the Print dialog box. If you click on the directory name above the list of files, you can use the path menu to view additional files. The Sorting option on the Commands menu is one of several devices designed to help you deal with long lists of documents meeting your criteria.

Searching for Documents Containing Particular Words

To have Word look *inside* each file on the disk being searched and list only those files containing a particular word or words:

1. Choose the Search button in the Find File dialog box to open the Search dialog box.
2. Choose the Advanced Search button to open the Advanced Search dialog box.
3. Enter the search string in the Containing Text box in the Summary tab of the Advanced Search dialog box.
   - Use the same care when specifying search text that you use with Word's Find and Replace commands.
   - Find File searches entire Word documents including headers, footers, and hidden text.

note

Several wildcards work here. For example, *Sm?th* will find both *Smith* and *Smyth*. The wild card ^W searches for white space. See on-line help for more about Find and Replace wildcards that can be used here too.

Finding Files Using Summary Info

If you and your colleagues have been religious about entering consistent Summary Information, you can use the Find File feature to search for those entries. Naturally, documents created with programs that do not collect Summary info (such as WordPerfect) will be ignored.

Footnotes

Footnotes are numbered notes placed at the bottom of the page to explain or expand upon body text. *Endnotes* are like footnotes but they appear at the end of a document or section.

To create footnotes:

1. Start by placing the insertion point where the footnote marker is needed.
2. Choose Insert ➤ Footnote.
3. Click OK to dismiss the Footnote and Endnote dialog box unless you want to use endnotes or other options.
4. If you are in Normal view, a second window pane opens where you do the footnote typing. In Page Layout view, you type right where the footnote will print—usually between the text and footer. Type the footnote.

5. To return to the main document, move the insertion point with the mouse or press Ctrl+Alt+Z.

Viewing Footnotes

Footnotes are always displayed in Page Layout view and Print Preview. If they are not visible in Normal or Outline view, choose View ➤ Footnotes to open the footnote pane.

To close the footnote pane, choose View ➤ Footnotes or click the Close button.

shortcut

Double-clicking on a footnote marker in your document will display the footnote pane and place the insertion point at the beginning of the footnote. If necessary, Word will open the footnote pane and scroll to the appropriate note. Moving the insertion point in the footnote pane will cause the main document to scroll to the reference.

Editing and Personalizing Footnotes

You can copy, move, or delete entire footnotes by working with the footnote marker in text using the same techniques you would any other character.

Editing Footnote Text

Visit the footnote pane in Normal view, or the footnote itself in Page Layout view. Cut, paste, and drag-and-drop away to your heart's content.

note

You cannot cut a footnote's entire text; you must cut the foot-note mark in text if you wish to delete or move it.

Format Painter

Word's new Format Painter feature gives you a quick way to copy formatting from one item to another. Here's how:

1. Select the text containing the formatting to copy.
2. To copy the formatting to one location, click once on the Standard toolbar button that looks like a paintbrush.
   - To copy to several locations, double-click.
3. When the mouse pointer changes to a paintbrush, select the text you wish to format.
4. If you double-clicked in step 2, press Escape when done, or click the Format Painter button again.

Formatting Characters

Use the toolbar buttons, keyboard shortcuts, the Font dialog box, or any combination thereof to format characters.

Formatting Characters with Toolbars

Select the text and use the character-formatting buttons (Font Size, Bold, Italic, Underline, etc.) on the Formatting toolbar.

Finding Out Which Character Formats Are at Work

Click the Help button on the Standard toolbar and point at the characters of interest. A balloon box will appear, containing information about the paragraph and character styling.

Changing Fonts and Font Sizes

Word makes it easy to change fonts and font sizes:

- Use the drop-down Font and Size lists on the Formatting toolbar.
- Type the name of the desired font or size directly into the Font or Size name boxes on the Formatting toolbar, then press ↵.
- Select Format ➤ Font and choose a font or size from the Font dialog box.

Increasing and Decreasing Font Size from the Keyboard

Use the keyboard shortcuts Ctrl+] and Ctrl+[to increase or decrease font size one point at a time or Ctrl+Shift-> and Ctrl+Shift-< to increase or decrease the font size by the standard increments listed in Word's various Font size lists.

Boldfacing Selected Text

Click the Bold button on the Formatting toolbar, use one of the keyboard shortcuts—Ctrl+B or Ctrl+Shift+B—or check the Bold check box in the Font Style list in Word's Font dialog box.

Italicizing Selected Text

Click the Italic button on the Formatting toolbar, use one of the keyboard shortcuts—Ctrl+I or Ctrl+Shift+I—or check the Italic check box in the Font Style list in Word's Font dialog box.

Underlining Selected Text

Click the Underline button on the Formatting toolbar (for single, continuous underline), use the keyboard shortcut—Ctrl+U—or choose one of the options in the Underline list in Word's Font dialog box.

Expanding or Condensing Selected Text

Open the Character Spacing tab in the Font dialog box (Format ➤ Font) and choose Expanded or Condensed from the Spacing list. Choose a point value to expand or condense by.

Creating Superscripts and Subscripts

Use the shortcuts Ctrl+= and Ctrl+Shift+= respectively, click the Superscript or Subscript buttons on the Formatting toolbar, or bring up the Character Spacing tab of the Font dialog box (Format ➤ Font) and choose either Raised or Lowered.

Changing Case of Selected Text

Use Format ➤ Change Case or press Shift+F3.

Formatting Paragraphs

Word paragraphs can be simple blank "lines" or complex collections of indentation, tab, line spacing and other settings. A paragraph's attributes are stored with its paragraph mark; deleting the mark removes a paragraph's formatting. To create new paragraphs, press the ↵ key.

Splitting One Paragraph into Two

Position the insertion point where you want to break the paragraph and press ↵. Watch out for extraneous spaces.

Joining Paragraphs

Select the paragraph mark that separates them and press the spacebar. Look out for extra spaces or tabs.

Forcing a New Line Without Creating a New Paragraph

Press Shift+↵. This inserts a *new line* mark, pushing text down to the next line, but does *not* create a new paragraph. This can be important when you are working with sophisticated styles.

Deleting a Paragraph

Double-click in the left margin to select the doomed paragraph, then press Backspace. This will delete the paragraph *and* its ¶ mark. Alternatively, you can select all text in the paragraph except the ¶ and delete it, which will leave the ¶ mark with its formatting information.

Modifying the Appearance of Paragraphs

Use the ruler, the Formatting toolbar, and the Paragraph dialog box (Format ➢ Paragraph) or one of Word's paragraph-formatting shortcut key combinations.

Indenting Paragraphs Automatically

Drag the top half of the triangular indent marker on the ruler to the right to the desired position; press Ctrl+M; or enter a setting in the First Line indent box in the Paragraph dialog box (Format ➢ Paragraph).

Increasing or Decreasing Indents by One Tab Stop

Use the Increase Indent and Decrease Indent buttons on the Formatting toolbar.

Using Hanging Indents

Drag the top half of the triangular indent marker to the left to the desired position; press Ctrl+T; or select First Line or Hanging in the Special drop-down list on the Indents and Spacing tab of the Paragraph dialog box(Format ➢ Paragraph) and enter a measurement in the By: box.

shortcut

Alternatively, click the Numbered (list) button or the Bullets (list) button on the Formatting toolbar, which automatically creates a hanging indent.

tip

To unhang a hanging indent, press Ctrl+Shift+T.

Specifying Paragraph Alignment

Use one of the four paragraph-alignment buttons on the Formatting toolbar (Left, Right, Center or Justify).

Using Other Paragraph-Formatting Tools

Visit the Paragraph dialog box (Format ➤ Paragraph) to see and use other paragraph-formatting options. Consult on-line help and the bigger books for details.

Frames

Frames let you precisely position objects virtually anywhere in your document. Frames can contain graphics, text, or both. Think of frames as pages within a page that you can move, resize, and embellish.

Inserting Empty Frames

Choose Insert ➤ Frame (or click the Insert Frame button on the Drawing toolbar). If you're in Page Layout view, click and drag to insert the frame. If you're in Normal view, Word will invite you to switch to Page Layout view so that you can see what you're doing. If you decline, it'll insert the frame as it thinks best.

Framing Existing Graphics or Other Elements

First select the object, then choose Insert ➤ Frame (or click the Insert Frame button on the Drawing toolbar).

Resizing Framed Items

Click the item to select the frame and display *handles* around it, then drag one of the handles to resize it.

Repositioning Frames

Place the mouse pointer along a side of the frame, hold down the mouse button and drag the frame to where you want to reposition it, then release the mouse button. To position frames precisely, enter measurements in the Frame dialog box (Format ➤ Frame).

Placing Text in a Frame (Captioning)

Select the frame and press ↵. Then just type away, stylizing the text as you like. The caption will stay with the frame when you move it.

Deleting a Frame and its Contents

Select the frame and press Ctrl+X or hit Backspace.

Removing a Frame from an Object

Select the frame, choose Format ➤ Frame to reach the Frame dialog box, then click the Remove Frame button.

Full Screen

To entirely clear the screen of everything but text, choose View ➤ Full Screen. To return to the prior view, click on the little Full button.

Go To

Go To lets you scoot quickly to a particular page or to a specific page within a certain section.

1. Press F5 or choose Edit ➤ Go To.
2. Type the desired page number in the Goto dialog box.
3. Press ↵. Word will take you to the requested page.
4. Close the Go To dialog box with the Close button or close box or press Esc.
5. Get back to work.

You can also use the Go To command to move forward or backward a specific number of pages. And you can use it to go to the end of a document, even if you don't know the last page number.

Here's a list of things you can do with the Go To dialog box and samples of typical entries.

- Move to the beginning of the document (0).
- Move to the next page (+ or leave blank).
- Move to the last page (enter any number greater than the number of pages in the document).
- Move to a specific page number (4 or P4)
- Move to a specific page within a specific section (P4S3)
- Move to the first page of a specific section (S3)
- Move forward a specified number of pages—3, for example (+3)
- Move back a specific number of pages—5, for instance (–5)

tip

You can also use Goto to move between a bunch of different Word items—Page, Section, Line, Bookmark, Annotation, Footnote, Endnote, Field, Table, Graphic, Equation, or Object—by selecting them in the drop-down list in the Goto dialog box.

Go Back

Word remembers the last three places you have edited plus the current insertion-point location. The Go Back feature lets you quickly move to those edit points. Press Shift+F5 (or Ctrl+Alt+Z) repeatedly to cycle you through the last four insertion-point locations.

Headers and Footers

You can have identical headers and footers on all pages in your document or you can specify different contents for each section of the document. Odd and even pages can have different designs if you wish. The first page of each document or each section can be unique.

You always edit headers and footers in Page Layout view. You work right in the header and footer area of your document after double-clicking to un-dim it or selecting View ➤ Header and Footer.

Apply virtually any paragraph or character style using the Formatting toolbar and rulers in headers and footers. You can also place framed items and frame anchors in headers or footers. They will repeat on all pages thereafter.

Use your regular document ruler or Formatting toolbar when working in header and footer windows. Margins, indents, tabs, and all the other tools work as you'd expect.

Using Even and Odd Headers and Footers

1. Place the insertion point in the section where you want the odd/even effect to begin (see *Sections* on page 97 for more info on sections).
2. Open the Page Setup dialog box (double-click in a blank part of the ruler or choose File ➤ Page Setup).
3. Visit the Layout tab.
4. Check the Different Odd and Even choice in the Headers and Footers area, then click OK.

Creating Different First Page Headers and Footers

1. Place the insertion point in the section where you want the different first page effect to begin.
2. Open the Page Setup dialog box (double-click in a blank part of a ruler or choose File ➤ Page Setup).
3. Choose the Layout tab.
4. Check the Different First Page choice in the Headers and Footers area. You'll have different header and footer areas on first pages. Their names will be visible in Page Layout view.
5. Create different headers and footers for the first page in Page Layout view.

Numbering Pages in Headers and Footers

Word offers a variety of tools to help you automatically number pages and many page numbering format and style choices. You can position page numbers nearly anywhere that pleases you.

If you plan to break a document into multiple sections, you may want to insert page numbers *before* you split the document into sections. Otherwise, you will have to repeat the page-numbering process for each section of your document.

Word provides two page-numbering techniques. Both have advantages and disadvantages. Normally, you will use only one for a particular document. Otherwise, you might end up with two or more sets of page numbers!

Numbering Pages with the Header and Footer Toolbar

1. Open a header or footer by double-clicking on it in Page Layout view or by selecting View ➤ Header and Footer.
2. Click on the page numbering button in the Header and Footer toolbar to insert a number at the insertion point.
3. Like anything else placed in headers and footers, page numbers can be stylized, repositioned, surrounded with borders, accompanied by text, and otherwise embellished.

Word uses the standard header or footer style to format page numbers placed therein. You can override this by applying additional character and paragraph formats or by changing the standard header or footer style (see *Styles and the Style Gallery* on page 104).

Headers and footers have tab stops, which you may find useful for positioning page numbers.

Numbering Pages with Insert ➤ Page Numbers

Insert ➤ Page Numbers provides a wide variety of numbering options. It reveals the Page Numbers dialog box and lets you quickly reach the Page Number Format dialog box.

1. Place the insertion point in the section to number.
2. Display the Page Numbering dialog box by choosing Insert ➤ Page Numbers.
3. Word suggests page numbers in the bottom-right corner of your document (½" from the bottom and right edges of the paper), but you can specify different positions

with the Position and Alignment drop-down menus. Watch the Preview area as you work.

4. Choose to place a page number on the first page or not by checking or unchecking the corresponding box.
5. Either click OK or click on the Format button to review other page numbering options.

Managing Starting Page Numbers

Word gives you four options for controlling the starting page number:

- Suppress the page number on the first page.
- Start each new section in a multisection document with 1.
- Suppress the page number on the first page and start the second page with 1.
- Use a number other than 1 for the first page, like 25 or 100.

note

In all the following examples, we assume that your document does not already have page numbers.

Suppressing the First Page Number

1. Place the insertion point in the desired section.
2. Open the Page Numbers dialog box (Insert ➤ Page Numbers).
3. Uncheck the Show Number on First Page box
4. Click OK.

Restarting Sections with 1

To restart each section at page 1, follow these steps:

1. Place the insertion point in any section. Open the Page Number dialog box (Insert ➤ Page Numbers).
2. Click on the Format button to reach the Page Number Format dialog box.
3. Check the Start At box.
4. Specify the number each section will start with (1 in this example).
5. Click OK in the Page Number Format dialog box, then again in the Page Number dialog box.

Suppressing the Page Number on the First Page and Starting the Second Page with 1

1. Choose Insert ➤ Page Numbers.
2. Uncheck the Show Number on First Page check box.
3. Click the Format button to open the Page Number Format dialog box.
4. Enter **0** in the Start At box, then click OK.
5. Click OK in the Page Numbers dialog box.

Using a Number other than 1 for the First Page

1. Choose Insert ➤ Page Numbers.
2. Click the Format button to open the Page Number Format dialog box.
3. Enter the number in the Start At box, then click OK.
4. Click OK in the Page Numbers dialog box.

Indenting

See *Formatting Paragraphs* on page 38.

Indexing and Tables of Contents

Word will help you create a *table of contents* (TOC) for your documents. If you format your headings using Word's standard heading styles or Outline feature, you can use Insert ➤ Index and Tables to quickly compile (create) a simple but very usable table of contents and place it in a new section at the beginning of your document.

You can also manually select items to appear in your table of contents.

Creating a Table of Contents

1. Begin by formatting your document's headings with Word's standard-heading styles. (These styles can be added to your Formatting toolbar's drop-down style list by visiting the Style dialog box. Be sure to hold down Shift when clicking on the Formatting toolbar's style drop-down list. See *Styles and the Style Gallery* on page 104.)
2. When you have typed and proofed your document and are happy with margins, headers, footers, and other design elements (especially those that affect page breaks), pick Insert ➤ Index and Tables.
3. Make sure the Table of Contents tab is foremost.
4. Preview the available formats by clicking in the Formats list and watching the Preview area. Pick one.
5. Choose the number of levels to include in the TOC.

6. If you wish to include a tab leader (dashes or dots, for instance), choose the style from the drop-down list.
7. Click OK or press Enter. Word will compile the new TOC. It starts by repaginating your document. Then it will the TOC at the insertion point.

If you've already created a TOC for the document, Word will ask if you want to replace it. If you choose No, you will end up with *two* TOCs at the beginning of your document. This is a way to create two levels of content detail like the Contents at a Glance and regular TOC at the beginning of some books.

Updating a Table of Contents

1. Click in the TOC to highlight the entire TOC (it will turn gray).
2. Click the right mouse button and select Update Fields from the shortcut menu.
3. Choose Update Page Numbers only or Entire Table.
4. Click OK.

Creating an Index

Automatic indexes are created using hidden codes sometimes called *XE* or *Index Entry* codes. Word compiles indexes on demand and places them at the end of your document in new sections that it creates for this purpose. Index entries can include the contents of headers and footers if you wish.

Marking Index Entries

You can create simple indexes by selecting text, pressing Alt+Shift+X, and choosing a few options. Word then compiles and stylizes an index and places it at document's end:

1. Proof and finalize margins, page endings, etc.
2. Select (highlight) a word or phrase you want to use as an index entry.
3. Press Alt+Shift+X. You'll see the Mark Index Entry dialog box.
4. Click Mark to mark just this entry, or Mark All to mark all occurrences. (Word will scan the document, mark all occurrences and the status area will tell you how many were found.) Edit the entry, and add a subentry. You can also include a cross reference at this time (see *Cross Referencing* on page 17).
5. The Mark Index dialog box remains visible so that you can scroll to other text and mark it, or simply type words to be indexed into the Main Entry section of the dialog box.
6. Repeat steps 2 through 6 until you have specified all desired entries.
7. Click on Close to close the dialog box.
8. Place the insertion point where you want the index (typically at the end of your document).
9. Choose Insert ➤ Index and Tables and make sure the Index tab is foremost in the Index and Tables dialog box.
10. Pick an index style using the scrolling Preview area as your guide. Double-click on the name of the desired style or click once on a style name and once on OK. Word will repaginate the document, then create an index that will be placed at the insertion point.

Updating Indexes

Each time you visit and close the Index tab in the Index and Tables dialog box, Word will ask if you want to replace (recompile) the selected index. Click Yes if you do.

shortcut

Click anywhere in the index to select it, right-click to see the shortcut menu, and choose Update Field. Word will repaginate, then recompile and update the index.

Insert Page Breaks

Page breaks are the places in your document where one page ends and a new page begins. Word makes them automatically, and you can force your own "manual" breaks.

1. Move the insertion point to where you want the break.
2. Choose Insert ➤ Break. You'll see the Break dialog box.
3. Make sure the Page Break button is selected (the default).
4. Click OK or tap the ↵ key. The Break dialog box will disappear and you'll see a thick manual page break line on your screen. Text or graphics below the manual page break will appear on the next page of your document.

Moving and Deleting Page Breaks

You can highlight and delete manual breaks like text in Normal and Outline views. (You cannot delete automatic breaks placed by Word.)

Inserting One File into Another

Place the insertion point where you want to insert the contents of a file. Choose Insert ➤ File and locate the file you wish to insert. Word will convert the document from other formats if necessary. You may need to clean-up the resulting insertion (by applying styles, and so on).

Linking and Embedding

Word 6's Object Linking and Embedding capabilities let you include in your Word documents information created in other applications.

When you *link* objects, the Word document stores the location of the object and its source application in a field; the object is saved in its source application. *Embedded* objects become part of the Word document and are stored in it.

To link an object created in another application to a Word file, you need to be running both applications in the same environment (e.g., in Windows with MS-DOS). Both applications must support either Object Linking and Embedding (OLE) or Dynamic Data Exchange (DDE). If you're not sure about all this, see the big books for details.

Linking an Object

1. Create or open the source application file containing the object.
2. Select the object and copy it to the Clipboard.
3. Switch back to Word and select Edit ➤ Paste Special.

4. In the Paste Special dialog box, choose the Paste Link option and click OK.

tip

To display an embedded or linked object as an icon instead of at its full size, check the Display as Icon check box in the Paste Special dialog box or Object dialog box when embedding or linking the object.

Editing Linked Objects

Double-click the object in the Word document. The source application opens with the object displayed ready for editing. You may not always want your Word documents to be updated automatically when the source objects change. Consider your alternatives.

Updating Linked Objects

You can update linked objects automatically or manually by choosing the Automatic or Manual option buttons in the Links dialog box (Edit ➤ Links).

note

When you choose Automatic updating, Word updates links whenever you open the document, and if the source file changes while you've got Word open.

To update links manually, choose Edit ➤ Links, select the links to be updated in the Links dialog box, and click the Update Now button.

tip

To update linked objects every time you print, select Tools ➤ Options to display the Options dialog box, select the Print tab, check the Update Links check box, then click OK.

Breaking a Link

Select Edit ➤ Links to open the Links dialog box, select the link or links that you want to break, and choose the Break Link button. Word will display a dialog box asking if you are sure. Select Yes.

shortcut

To break a link quickly, select it in your document and press Ctrl+Shift+F9.

warning

You can't reconnect a broken link (except by using Edit ➤ Undo *immediately*).

Locking and Unlocking Links

Select Edit ➤ Links to open the Links Dialog box, select the link or links that you want to lock or unlock, and check the Locked check box to lock them or uncheck it to unlock them.

shortcut

To lock links quickly, select the links in your document and press Ctrl+F11. To unlock links, press Ctrl+Shift+F11.

Reconnecting Lost Links

Choose Edit ➤ Links to open the Links dialog box, choose the link to reconnect, choose the Change Source button, and select the file to which you want to reconnect the link.

Embedding Objects in Your Documents

Open in the source application the file containing the object, then select the object and copy it to the Clipboard. Switch back to Word and paste in the object.

Editing an Embedded Object

Double-click the object to open the application in which the object was created. Edit the object, then select File ➤ Exit and Return to quit the source application and return to Word.

Changing an Embedded Object's Source Application

Select Edit ➤ Object, choose the object you want to convert, and select Convert from the extension menu. Then select the Convert To button to permanently convert the embedded object, or select the Activate As button to temporarily convert the embedded object to the format you specify.

Removing an Embedded Object

Select the object and press Delete.

Macros

A *macro* is a series of Word commands grouped together as a single command to make everyday tasks easier. You can assign a macro to a toolbar, menu, or shortcut keys and run it by simply clicking a button, selecting a menu choice, or pressing a key combination. You can create a macro in two ways:

- Record a series of actions using the keyboard and mouse. This is the easiest way.
- Type a macro directly into a macro-editing window. This way you have more flexibility, and can include WordBasic instructions that you can't record using the keyboard and mouse.

tip

When creating complicated macros, record as much as possible and then edit the results.

Recording Macros

1. Start the macro recorder by double-clicking REC on the status bar. The Record Macro dialog box will appear.
2. Enter a name for the macro in the Record Macro Name box. If you don't give your macro a name, Word will name it Macro1, Macro2, and so on. No spaces, commas, or periods allowed in the name.
3. Enter a description of what the macro does in the Description box. This is optional but heavily recommended. Use up to 255 characters.
4. To assign the macro to a toolbar, a menu, or a keyboard shortcut, click the Toolbars, Menus, or Keyboard button.
5. If your current document is attached to a template other than NORMAL.DOT, drop down the Save Changes In list and select either that template or Normal.
6. Click OK. The Macro dialog box will disappear, but the Macro toolbar will appear on your screen. Perform the actions you want to record.
   - The Macro toolbar contains 12 buttons and a name box. Hold the mouse pointer over a button to learn its name and function.
7. To stop recording the macro, click the Stop button on the Macro Record toolbar. The Macro Record toolbar will disappear.

tip

You can also start the macro recorder by selecting Tools ➤ Macro, then clicking the Record button in the Macro dialog box; or by clicking the Record button on the Macro toolbar.

Pausing While Recording a Macro

1. Click the Pause button on the Macro Record toolbar to pause recording.
2. Perform the actions you don't want to record.
3. Click the Pause button again to restart recording (just like a tape recorder!).

Editing a Macro

1. Select Tools ➤ Macro. The Macro dialog box will appear.
2. Select the list of macros to choose from by dropping down the Macros Available In box.
3. Choose the macro you want to edit, then click the Edit button. The macro-editing window will appear, displaying the text of the macro you chose.
4. Edit the macro. (See the big books for details.)

Creating a Macro in the Macro-Editing Window

1. Choose Tools Macro to open the Macro dialog box.
2. Enter a name for the macro in the Macro Name box.
3. Click the Create button to open the macro-editing window. The Macro toolbar will appear.
4. Enter the macro text between the *Sub MAIN* and *End Sub* lines that mark the beginning and end of the macro.
5. When you're finished, close the macro-editing window (File ➤ Close) and save changes.

Running a Macro

Once you have recorded your macro, you can assign it to a toolbar, a menu, or a shortcut key combination. You can then run it as you would a normal Word command or feature.

If you don't want to assign a macro to a toolbar, menu, or key combination—perhaps you simply have too many macros, or use some of them too seldom to merit having them available all the time—you can also run a macro by highlighting the name of the macro in the Macro dialog box (Tools ➤ Macro) and clicking the Run button.

If you've got everything right, your macro will perform the actions you taught it to do. If something is wrong, you may have to edit it.

Deleting a Macro

1. Select Tools ➤ Macro to open the Macro dialog box.
2. Highlight the macro to delete.
3. Click the Delete button. Confirm your intention.
4. Click the Close button to return to your document.

Mail Merge

Word's Mail Merge function lets you produce form letters (like those lovely ones you get from Publishers Clearing House), envelopes, mailing labels, and things like parts lists and catalogs.

new in Word 6

Mail merges used to be scary and confusing at best, but Word 6's new Mail Merge Helper makes the process so painless you might even find yourself merging for fun.

What You Need for a Mail Merge

To perform a merge, you need a *main document*, which contains the text of the document to be generated and fields in which to insert information; and a *data source*, which contains the records to be inserted into the fields in the main document.

Running a Mail Merge

1. Select Tools ➤ Mail Merge to start the Mail Merge Helper.
2. Start your main document for the merge by selecting the Create button in the Mail Merge Helper dialog box and choosing the type of document from the drop-down list.
   - Word will ask if you want to use the Active Window or a New Main Document. Use the Active Window unless you've got something important there.
3. Specify the data source for the merge by clicking the Get Data button in the Mail Merge Helper dialog box and choosing whether to open an existing data source or create a new data source.
4. Use the Create Data Source dialog box to add fields to the Header Row for the merge.
   - To add a field name, type it in the Field Name box and click Add.

- To remove a field name, highlight it in the Field Names in Header Row box and click Remove.
- To rearrange the field names in the Field Names in Header Row box, highlight a name and click the Move arrows.

5. Click OK when you're done. The Save Data Source dialog box will appear. This works just like the Save As dialog box (see Save on page for more details).
6. Word will then invite you to add records to your data source or add merge fields to your main document. Choose the Edit Data Source button.
7. In the Data Form dialog box, enter the records (information) for the fields you arranged in the Create Data Source dialog box.
   - Press Tab to move forwards between fields; Shift-Tab to move backwards.
   - Click the Add New button to add another record.
   - Click the Delete button to delete a record.
   - Use the First, Previous, Next, and Last buttons in by the Records box to move between records.
8. Click OK when you're done. Word will open your main document with the Mail Merge toolbar displayed.
9. Enter the text of your main document, then insert merge fields and Word fields in your main document by clicking the buttons to drop down lists of fields, then selecting fields from the list.
   - Merge fields will insert information from your data source in your document.
   - Word fields insert instructions to Word on handling the merge. See the big books for details.

10. Reopen the Mail Merge Helper by clicking the Mail Merge Helper button on the Mail Merge toolbar or by selecting Tools Mail Merge again.
11. If you want to sort merged documents, choose the Query Options button in the Mail Merge Helper dialog box. In the Query Options dialog box, click the Sort Records tab. Enter your sorting choices in the Sort By field and the Then By fields, then click OK.
12. If you want to filter merged documents, choose the Query Options button in the Mail Merge Helper dialog box. In the Query Options dialog box, click the Filter Records tab. Enter your filtering choices in the Field and Comparison columns. Choose And or Or in the second row to continue the filtering. Then click OK.
13. You're now ready to merge your documents. Choose the Merge button in the Mail Merge Helper dialog box to display the Merge dialog box.
    - Choose whether to send the merged documents to a printer or a new file. (If you send them to a file, you can check that everything's OK before printing them.)
    - Choose which records to merge
    - Decide whether to print blank lines (probably not).
14. Click OK. Word will merge your documents, then display the resulting document (if you chose to merge to a new file).
15. Edit, print, and save your merged documents.

note

Word will invite you to save your main file and data documents. You'll probably want to do so.

Merging Labels, Envelopes, or Catalogs

Choose Mailing Labels, Envelopes, or Catalog from the Create drop-down list in the Mail Merge Helper dialog box.

Consult the bigger books and on-line help for more information on merging tools and techniques.

Margins and Gutters

You can use one set of margin and gutter settings for an entire document, or you can define different settings for different pages in your document.

note

To use different margin settings on different pages, you need to use sections. See *Sections* on page 97 for more information.

reminder

Indents are *added* to margin settings. That is to say, if you specify a 1.0" left margin and a ½" left indent, your text will print 1½" from the left edge of the page. If you set a 1.0" right margin and indent the right edge of a paragraph 1.0", the text will stop 2.0" from the right edge of the page.

Changing Document Margins

Word gives you three ways to change margins:

- Select File ➤ Page Setup to open the Page Setup dialog box. Choose the Margins tab and specify margins.
- Drag new margins with the rulers in Page Layout view. The margin brackets are located on the ruler.
- Drag margins using the rulers in Print Preview.

Using Facing (Mirror) Margins

Select the Mirror Margins feature in the Margins tab of the Page Setup dialog box (File ➤ Page Setup) when you want different left and right margin widths and your final output will be two-sided. Word makes inside margins of odd- and even-numbered pages the same size, and does the same with the outside margins of odd and even pages. This is how you get white space on the appropriate side of even and odd, two-sided pages.

warning

When adjusting margins in Print Preview, if you've chosen the Mirror Odd/Even feature, display two pages so that you know if you're working with an odd or even page.

Specifying Gutters to Facilitate Binding

Gutters are additional white space in the inside margins. The gutter width, which you specify in the Margin tab of the Page Setup dialog box (File ➤ Page Setup), reduces the text area.

Numbered Lists

See *Bullets* (page 12).

Numbering Pages

See *Headers and Footers* on page 44.

Objects

See *Linking and Embedding* on page 53.

Options

Word gives you a great deal of control over its various options. For example, you can dictate default view settings, menu appearance, default font settings, and much more. Many of these choices are made using Tools ➤ Options and the tabs in the Options dialog box. These choices apply to *all* your Word templates.

Choices made using Tools ➤ Customize and the tabs in the Customize dialog box are *template specific*—they apply only to the template in which you arrange them. This means you could have NORMAL.DOT and all documents based on it display the default Word menus, toolbars, and so on, but have your CLEVERME and SPESHL4U templates and their documents display customized menus and toolbars.

View Options

The View tab lets you control what you see in your document. For instance, if you want to see hidden text, check the Hidden Text check box.

Draft Font

The Draft Font choice is for Outline and Normal views and determines whether Word displays your prose in the fonts you've chosen or in its draft font.

Wrap to Window

Wrap to Window wraps the text from one line to the next within the document window. Use this when you need to work with several windows visible on your desktop at the same time and you don't want your text to be wider than the window.

Picture Placeholders

To speed scrolling in documents containing graphics, mark the Picture Placeholders check box to display graphics as empty boxes.

Field Codes

You'll probably want to view field codes rather than field results when you're inserting and editing fields. Simply check the check box. Field codes look something like this:

```
{ EDITTIME \* MERGEFORMAT }
```

Bookmarks

Check the Bookmarks check box to display the bookmarks and links your document contains. Bookmarks appear in square gray brackets.

Field Shading

When you're working with a document that contains fields, you can choose to have their results shaded so you can avoid changing them by mistake—remember, the results may look like regular text. Choose from When Selected (when the insertion point is in the field), Always, and Never.

Status Bar

If you find the information on the status bar confusing, or if you simply need more space on your screen for displaying your immortal words in huge point sizes, uncheck this box to remove the status bar.

Horizontal Scroll Bar

If you never use the horizontal scroll bar, you can remove it by unchecking the check box.

Vertical Scroll Bar

If you always use the keyboard for moving through your documents, you may want to remove the vertical scroll bar from your screen to give yourself a bit more space. Simply uncheck the box and it'll be gone.

Style Area Width

The style area is the area to the left of the text that shows the applied style names. To display it, enter a positive decimal measurement, such as 0.5". To rid the display of the style area, enter 0 (zero).

Tab Characters

Check the Tab Characters check box to display tabs as right-pointing arrows. You may want to do this if you're aligning things and can't be bothered to use tables.

Spaces

Check the Spaces check box to display spaces entered with the spacebar as dots about halfway up the height of the line. This helps you find double or triple spaces in proportional fonts.

Paragraph Marks

Check the Paragraph Marks check box to display hard returns entered with ↵ as ¶. This can be especially useful when you're editing a document that uses styles and deleting the wrong paragraph mark inadvertently will apply the wrong style to your text.

Optional Hyphens

Optional hyphens—the ones you insert to indicate where to break a word if it falls at the end of a line—are normally not displayed. To display them, check the Optional Hyphens check box.

Hidden Text

To view hidden text, check the Hidden Text check box. It will appear as text with a dotted underline. Remember that while viewing hidden text will change the line breaks and pagination of your document, hidden text will not print unless you've selected the Hidden Text option in the Include with Document area on the Print tab in the Options dialog box.

All

Check this check box to display all the nonprinting characters—tabs, spaces, paragraph marks, optional hyphens, and hidden text. (If you don't always want these displayed, you can get the same effect by clicking the Show/Hide ¶ button on the Standard toolbar.)

General Options

The options on the General tab modify Word settings such as the default units of measurement and the display of three-dimensional effects.

Background Repagination

Word automatically repaginates your documents as you work, computing new lines and page endings whenever you are not typing. Uncheck this box to disable automatic repagination.

Help for WordPerfect Users

The Help for WordPerfect Users check box will be selected if you agreed to have it active when you installed Word. With this option selected, Word displays information or demonstrates a command when you press a WordPerfect for DOS key combination in Word.

Navigation Keys for WordPerfect Users

Check the Navigation Keys for WordPerfect Users check box to change the functions of the Page Up, Page Down, Home, End, and Esc keys to their WordPerfect equivalents. This disables those keys' regular functions for Word.

Blue Background, White Text

Check this check box to display the text as white characters on a blue background.

Beep on Error Actions

When the Beep on Error Actions check box is checked, Word will beep when you make a mistake.

3D Dialog and Display Effects

The 3D Dialog and Display Effects check box controls the appearance of the dialog boxes. Turn this off for quicker screen updates.

Update Automatic Links at Open

The Update Automatic Links at Open check box is one you might seriously consider unchecking. When it's checked, any information in a document that's linked to other files is updated every time you open the document.

Mail As Attachment

Check the Mail As Attachment check box to attach documents to a mail message. You need to have an e-mail program installed on your computer to use this option.

Recently Used File List

The Recently Used File List box controls the number of your last-used files that appear at the bottom of the File menu. Choose between 0 and 9.

Measurement Units

Pull down the Measurement Units list and choose Inches, Centimeters, Points, or Picas as the default measurement unit for Word. You may want to choose Points or Picas if you're typesetting things.

Edit Options

The Edit tab is where you control a whole bunch of important options that affect the way you work, such as whether what you type will replace a selection or bump it along, how Word handles drag-and-drop editing, and whether Word worries about extra spaces when you use cut and paste.

Typing Replaces Selection

With the Typing Replaces Selection check box checked, any text you've selected gets deleted as soon as you start typing. This saves you the step of deleting a selection when you want to replace it; but if your mind doesn't work that way and you find this option awkward, uncheck the check box. Then selected text will be bumped along to the right when you type something.

Drag-and-Drop Text Editing

Drag and drop lets you move or copy selected text without pasting it to the Clipboard. If you never use it, turn it off by unchecking the Drag-and-Drop Text Editing check box.

Automatic Word Selection

When the Automatic Word Selection check box is checked, Word selects the entire word (*including any trailing space at the end*) when you select any part of it by dragging the mouse pointer from the previous word. Uncheck the check box to turn this off.

Use the INS Key for Paste

Check the Use the INS Key for Paste check box if you get tired of pressing Shift+Ins to insert the contents of the Clipboard into your document.

Overtype Mode

Check the Overtype Mode check box to have Overtype mode turned on by default when you use Word.

Use Smart Cut and Paste

Check the Use Smart Cut and Paste check box to have Word automatically remove extra spaces when you delete text or add spaces when you insert text.

Allow Accented Uppercase

Check the Allow Accented Uppercase check box if you're working with text formatted as French and you want to allow the spelling and grammar checkers to suggest that Word add an accent mark to an uppercase letter.

Picture Editor

Select the application you want to use as a picture editor from the drop-down list. Your choices will depend on what's loaded on your machine.

Print Options

The Print tab allows you to make some vital settings. You can decide to print backwards; you can make sure fields and links get updated before you print; and you can print annotations and hidden text with your document.

Draft Output

Check the Draft Output check box to print your documents with minimal formatting. This option provides faster printing.

Reverse Print Order

Check the Reverse Print Order check box to print your documents starting at the last page.

Update Fields

Make sure the Update Fields check box is checked if you want all fields in your document (for example, date fields and page numbers) to be updated whenever you print.

Update Links

Check the Update Links check box to have all links in your document updated every time you print. If the sources for your links are apt to change or be unavailable, leave this box unchecked.

Background Printing

Check the Background Printing check box if you want to be able to continue working in Word while you print a document.

Summary Info

Check the Summary Info check box to have Word print file summary information on a separate page after printing the document.

Field Codes

Check the Field Codes check box to have Word print the field codes rather than the field results in the document.

Annotations

Check the Annotations check box to have Word print out a document's annotations on a separate page at the end of the document.

Hidden Text

Check the Hidden Text check box to have Word print out any hidden text the document contains. Hidden text will look like normal text when printed; Word doesn't print the dotted underline you see for hidden text on the screen. Bear in mind that printing hidden text will affect line and page breaks in your document; if that matters to you, view hidden text on screen before printing it, and do any necessary fiddling with line and page breaks.

Drawing Objects

Check the Drawing Objects check box to have Word print drawing objects (for example charts, graphics, and equations) created in Word with the document.

Print Data Only on Forms

Check the Print Data Only on Forms check box to print only the information entered in form fields in a form—not the form itself. You might want to use this for filling in preprinted forms.

note

This option applies only to the current document, not to all documents.

Default Tray

Choose a default paper tray from the drop-down list. The default setting is From Control Panel, since that's where you'll probably set printing options for all your Windows applications. If you want to use different paper sources for different sections of documents (for example, if you're printing an envelope and a letter), use File ➤ Page Setup.

Options for Revision Marks

Word 6 lets different reviewers on the same document use different-colored revision marks. Choose Tools ➤ Options and select the Revisions tab of the Options dialog box to specify the revision options you want.

Inserted Text

Drop down the list for the Mark option and select the format with which you want mark new text. Choose from none, Bold, Italic, Underline, and Double Underline.

Color for New Text

Drop down the list for the Color for New Text option and select the color with which you want to mark new text. Choose By Author for automatic choice of colors by Word for the first eight people to revise the document (after that, Word starts over with the colors), or choose one of the colors manually.

Mark Deleted Text

Use the Mark drop-down list to select how you want to display text you are deleting from the document. Choose Hidden or Strikethrough.

Color for Deleted Text

Drop down the Color list and select the color with which you want to mark deleted text. Choose By Author for automatic choice of colors by Word for the first eight people to revise the document (after that, Word starts over with the colors), or choose one of the colors manually.

Mark Revised Lines

Drop down the Mark list and select how to mark revised lines: None, Left Border, Right Border, or Outside Border (the default).

Color for Revised Lines

Drop down the list and select the color with which to mark revised lines. Choose By Author for automatic choice of colors by Word for the first eight people to revise the document

User Info

The User Info tab specifies information about the primary user of the copy of Word you are using: the name, the return address for envelopes, and the initials to be used for annotations.

Name

Type the name for Word to use as the author in the summary information (File ➤ Summary Info) for documents you create. The default setting is the name entered when installing Word.

Initials

Enter the initials you want Word to use for annotation marks. The default setting is the initials entered for the name when installing Word.

Mailing Address

The Mailing Address area displays the return address used on envelopes once you've used the Create Envelope command. Until then, the default setting is the address entered when installing Word. Any address you enter here will be displayed as the return address in the Envelopes and Labels dialog box.

Compatibility Options

The options on the Compatibility tab determine how Word displays documents created either in earlier versions of Word or in other word-processing programs. Use these settings to make documents in Word 6 more closely match the original documents.

Font Substitution

Select the Font Substitution button to choose substitute fonts for fonts used in the active document that are not available on your computer.

Recommended Options For

Pull down the Recommended Options For drop-down list and select the word-processing application for which to set options. Select Custom to specify options for an unlisted application. In the list of Options, check the options you want to use.

File Locations

The File Locations tab of the Options dialog box lets you define where your documents, templates, and other items are stored by default.

Here are the default settings for options on the File Locations tab:

File Type	Default Location
Documents	C:\WINWORD
Clipart Pictures	C:\WINWORD\CLIPART
User Templates	C:\WINWORD\TEMPLATE
Workgroup Templates	(Depends on workgroup selections)
User Options	C:\WINWORD
AutoSave Files	(Depends on system settings)
Dictionaries	C:\WINWORD
Tutorial	C:\WINWORD\WORDCBT
Startup	C:\WINWORD\STARTUP

To set a new default location for an item, select the item and choose the Modify button. In the Modify Location dialog box, select the drive and directory for the item, and then click OK.

tip

You can create a new subdirectory by clicking the New button.

Save Options

The settings on the Save tab in the Options dialog box let you customize how and when you save your documents and choose protection for file sharing for the current document.

Always Create Backup Copy

Check the Always Create Backup Copy check box to have Word make automatic backups for you. Each time you save a document, Word saves a duplicate with a .BAK extension.

Allow Fast Saves

Check the Allow Fast Saves check box to speed up saving. Word then records only the changes to the document when you save it (rather than resaving the whole file).

Prompt for Summary Info

Check the Prompt for Summary Info check box to have Word display the Summary Info dialog box automatically whenever you save a new document.

Prompt to Save Normal.dot

Check the Prompt to Save Normal.dot check box if you want Word to consult you before saving changes you made to the default settings in your Word session when you exit Word. This box is unchecked by default, so Word automatically saves changes to NORMAL.DOT when you exit Word.

Save Native Picture Formats Only

Check the Save Native Picture Formats Only check box if you want to save only the Windows version of imported graphics. If you bring graphics into Word from another platform (for example, from the Macintosh), you can reduce the size of the Word document by storing only the version of the graphics that is native to Word.

Embed TrueType Fonts

Check the Embed TrueType Fonts check box if you want others who read the document on PCs that do not have the fonts used in it to be able to view it with the right fonts. If you're not sharing documents, leave this box unchecked.

Save Data Only for Forms

Check the Save Data Only for Forms check box to save the data in a form as a record you can use in a database. To save the data with the form, leave this box unchecked.

Automatic Save Every nn Minutes

Check the Automatic Save Every *nn* Minutes check box to have Word provide a safety net for you in the event of a power failure or computer crash. Don't rely upon this as your only backup. Make manual backups and store them off-site as well.

Protection Password

Enter a password (up to 15 characters; letters, spaces, symbols, and numbers are all okay) in the Protection Password text box to prevent other users from opening the current document.

warning

Case matters in passwords.

Write Reservation Password

Enter a password (up to 15 characters; letters, spaces, symbols, and numbers all OK) in the Write Reservation Password text box to prevent others from saving changes to the current document.

Read-Only Recommended

Check the Read-Only Recommended check box to recommend that others open the current document as read-only. (It's only a recommendation—they can disregard it.)

Spelling Options

The settings on the Spelling tab in the Options dialog box let you control the behavior of Word's spelling checker.

Always Suggest

Check the Always Suggest check box to have Word display suggested spellings for misspelled words it finds during a spelling check.

From Main Dictionary Only

Check the From Main Dictionary Only check box to have Word display suggested correct spellings from the main dictionary but not from any open custom dictionaries.

Words in UPPERCASE

Check the Words in UPPERCASE check box to have Word's spelling checker ignore words in which every character is uppercase. This is useful for working with technical terms, abbreviations, and so on.

Words with Numbers

Check the Words with Numbers check box to have Word's spell checker ignore any word that contains a number. This too is useful for working with technical terms and the like.

Reset Ignore All

Click the Reset Ignore All button to stop Word from ignoring the words you marked with Ignore All during the current Word session. This button isn't available till you've told Word to ignore all instances of a word.

Custom Dictionaries

Check any dictionary available here to activate it. You can then add words to it that aren't in the main dictionary when you run a spelling check.

New

Click the New button to display the Create Custom Dictionary dialog box and create a new custom dictionary that you can teach all the words that Word's main dictionary disagrees with. This way, you can have different dictionaries for different types of work.

Edit

Highlight a custom dictionary, and then click the Edit button to open it as a Word document so you can edit it.

Add

Click the Add button if you want to add a custom dictionary to the list for checking spelling.

Remove

To remove a custom dictionary from the Custom Dictionaries list, select it and click the Remove button.

Language

Pull down the Language list and choose a language to apply its formatting to a custom dictionary. Then Word will use that custom dictionary only when checking text formatted in that language. Format the dictionary as None to have Word use that dictionary when checking text formatted in any language.

Grammar

Here's where you get to choose which rules Word's grammar checker uses when critiquing your documents.

Use Grammar and Style Rules

Choose from Strictly (All Rules), For Business Writing, and For Casual Writing to define which rules Word uses when grammar-checking your documents. Choose Custom 1, Custom 2, or Custom 3 to set up your own rules without disturbing Word's preset offerings.

Customize Settings

Click the Customize Settings button to produce the Customize Grammar Settings dialog box, in which you can choose which rules to apply by default to your documents.

Check Spelling

Uncheck the Check Spelling check box (checked by default) if you don't want to check spelling in your documents while checking the grammar.

Show Readability Statistics

Uncheck the Show Readability Statistics check box (checked by default) if you don't want to see the Readability Statistics dialog box after each completed grammar check.

AutoFormat Options

The options on the AutoFormat tab let you set rules for Word to follow when it automatically formats text with the built-in styles. For example, you can instruct Word to replace straight quotes with smart quotes.

Previously Applied Styles

Check the Previously Applied Styles check box to have Word retain styles you applied when it automatically formats the document.

Headings

Check the Headings check box if you want Word to automatically apply Heading 1 through Heading 9 styles to headings.

Lists

Check the Lists check box if you want Word to automatically apply list and bullet styles to numbered, bulleted, and multilevel lists. Bear in mind that Word will automatically remove any manually inserted numbers or bullets in the process.

Other Paragraphs

Check the Other Paragraphs check box if you want Word to automatically apply paragraph styles other than the styles for headings and lists. For example, with Other Paragraphs checked, Word could apply Body Text style and so on.

Paragraph Marks

Check the Paragraph Marks check box if you want Word to standardize spacing in the document by removing paragraph marks it considers unnecessary (for example, a paragraph mark at the end of a line that would normally wrap) or adding paragraph marks it thinks your document is missing.

Tabs and Spaces

Check the Tabs and Spaces check box if you want Word to standardize spacing by replacing spaces with tabs and removing tabs and spaces it considers unnecessary.

Empty Paragraphs

Check the Empty Paragraphs check box if you want Word to standardize spacing by removing blank lines between paragraphs with certain styles—for example, between body text and body text.

Straight Quotes with Smart Quotes

Check the Straight Quotes with Smart Quotes check box if you want Word to replace " " with “ ” and ' ' with ‘ ’ when it formats your document.

Symbol Characters with Symbols

Check the Symbol Characters with Symbols check box if you want Word to replace characters used in place of symbols with symbols—for example, (TM) with ™, (R) with ®, and (C) with ©.

Bullet Characters with Bullets

Check the Bullet Characters with Bullets check box to have Word replace characters used as bullets (for example, * or +) with •.

Outlines

Outline view (View ➤ Outline or Ctrl+Alt+O) is a collection of tools designed to help you plan, create, and reorganize long documents. It does this by letting you expand or contract the amount of detail you see on your screen. Figure 1 illustrates this.

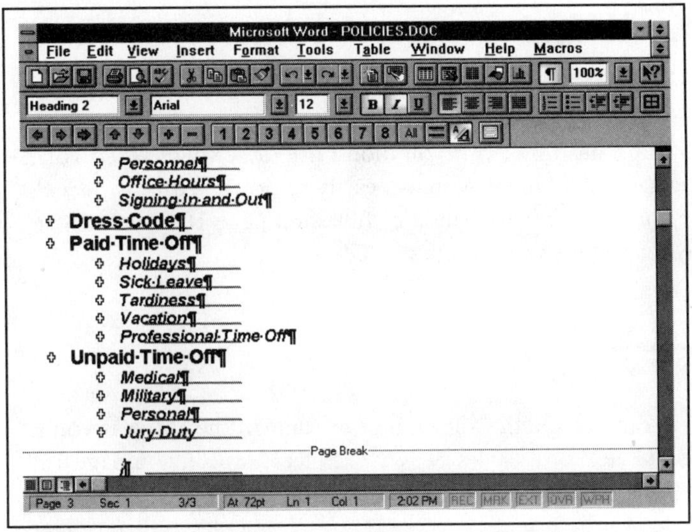

FIGURE 1: *Outline view lets you get a bird's-eye view of large documents.*

Figure 1 shows a document in Outline view, with all the body text collapsed (not revealed). Since only paragraph headings are visible in the bottom window, it's easy to see the overall organization (the outline) of the document. Outline view lets you control how much detail you see. For instance, you can view the first line of text following each heading if you wish.

Outline view provides a number of unique tools on the Outline toolbar at the top of the screen. The new compass-like pointer shape indicates the pointer's ability to move large collections of text.

As you can see in Figure 1, on-screen text is often underlined with an unusual line style. This does not indicate text that will be underlined when printed. Rather, it indicates that there is collapsed subtext beneath it.

note

In order to use Outline view, your headings need to be formatted using Word's standard heading styles (heading 1 through heading 9). If you didn't use these styles when you created a document, you can easily reformat with them. See *Applying Styles from the Formatting Toolbar* on page 104 and *Applying Styles from the Keyboard* on page 104.

tip

You can change the appearance of standard headings if you don't like Word's styles. See *Styles and the Style Gallery* on page 104.

Creating and Editing Outlines

When you start typing a new document in Outline view, Word assumes the first thing you want to type is a level 1 heading. Each new paragraph you type will take on the heading level of the previous paragraph.

Promoting and Demoting Headings

Use the two arrows at the left end of the Outline bar to promote and demote headings. Place the insertion point in the heading you wish to promote or demote, then click the right arrow to demote it or the left arrow to promote it.

Outlining Existing Documents

1. Open your document in Outline view. You will see the first line of each paragraph.
2. Place the insertion point in each heading and promote or demote them as described above.
3. Save your work.
4. Use the viewing techniques described next to view, rearrange and understand the organization of your document.

Expanding and Collapsing Outlines

To collapse a document's contents and get an overview, select the part of your document to collapse or expand and then click the + or - button on the Outline toolbar.

To expand or collapse an outline to a certain level of heading, click the appropriate numbered button (1–8).

Moving Paragraphs in Outline View

With the outline collapsed, you can move collections of paragraphs (also called *subtext*) by moving their associated headings. When you move a heading, *all* heads (i.e., those of lower head levels) and text below it will be moved along with it.

This lets you move entire chapters without needing to highlight them.

Placing the pointer over the left edge of a heading changes the pointer's shape. It will look like a compass. Click and drag, and a large right arrow will appear along with a dotted line. Drag the line and the pointer to where you want to move the text. Release the mouse button and the document will be reorganized.

The up- and down-pointing arrows on the Outline bar will also move items up and down. Highlight the headings, then click on the appropriate arrow.

Dragging to Change Outline Levels

You can also drag to change the indent level in Outline view. When you do, the pointer arrow changes to a guideline that indicates the pending indent level.

Numbering Headings in Outline View

You can number headings in Outline view, just as you can in any other view. The basic steps are:

1. Choose Format ➤ Heading Numbering.
2. Click on a sample to select the numbering format you desire, or choose Modify for custom numbering choices.
3. Click OK. Word will renumber immediately and whenever you rearrange your outline. Whenever you add a heading, it will automatically be numbered.

Using Outlines to Produce Tables of Contents

Since Outlines use (assign) standard Word heading styles to headings, you can quickly create a table of contents based on your outline. The TOC will include each heading from the outline.

Printing Outlines

Printing in Outline view creates a document containing only the levels you see on the screen. Collapse the document to the desired level, then select File ➤ Print (Ctrl+P).

warning

Even if just the first line of text appears, Word will print the whole paragraph.

Page Numbering

See *Headers and Footers* on page 44.

Print Preview

See *Views* on page 132.

Printing

Print as you would in any other Windows application. Begin by selecting a printer. Then choose File ➤ Print (Ctrl+P) and choose options in the Print dialog box. For quick printing of one copy of the entire document, use the Printer button on the Standard toolbar.

Replace

Replacing always starts by specifying what you want to find. (See Find on page 28 for details.) To replace, follow these general steps:

1. Save your work.
2. Choose Edit ➤ Replace or press Ctrl+H.
3. Create search criteria using the techniques discussed in Find (see page 28).
4. Specify the desired replacement text, formats, etc.
5. Tell Word where to search and in which direction.
6. Click Find Next or Replace All to start the replacement.
7. Confirm the replacements.

warning

Save your work before using the Replace feature.

The Replace dialog box looks like the Find dialog box, with additional features. Word lets you confirm each replacement before it happens, or it will find and replace without your intervention.

Just as you can search for text, formats, styles, and special characters, you can also replace them. You can even replace text with graphics.

Replacing Text with Text

1. Save your work.
2. Choose Edit ➤ Replace (Ctrl+H).
3. Visit the Search drop-down menu to tell Word if you want it to search the entire document, upwards, or downwards.
   - To search only a part of your document, select that part before choosing Edit ➤ Replace.

warning

If there are any formats or styles listed under the Find What or Replace With boxes, click No Formatting with the insertion point in the appropriate place (Find What, Replace With, or both). This way, Word will not alter the style or format of the document.

4. When the replacement instructions are complete, click Find Next. Word will search the document (or selected portion) for things matching your Find criteria and propose the next replacement. The Replace button should undim, and your document screen should scroll to reveal the first potential replacement point.

5. If you want Word to make the change it is proposing, click Replace. To skip the change, click Find Next. To make the change and let Word continue uninterrupted, click Replace All. Word will make the rest of the replacements non-stop, and probably too quickly for you to even see them, and will then give you a dialog box telling you how many replacements it made. Click OK.
6. Check your work.

Replacing Formatting

1. Specify the character attributes you want Word to find (italics, for example). Place the insertion point in the Find What entry box. Then specify Italic either from the Standard toolbar; or pull down the Format list in the Replace dialog box, choose Font, then check the Italic option in the Font dialog box. The word *Italic* (or whatever) will appear beneath the Find What box.
2. Go to the Replace With box and specify the new format (Underline in this example). To prevent Word from changing the italic to italic underline, you may need to click the Formatting toolbar's italic button until the Replace With criteria read *Not Italic: Underline.*
3. Perform the replace as decribed in the previous section.

shortcut

You can use keyboard shortcuts or toolbar buttons to specify formatting in the Find What and Replace With boxes. This is often much quicker.

Replacing Styles

To change the style of certain paragraphs, use Edit ➤ Replace:

1. Click on the Format button.
2. Choose Styles. You'll see a list of your document's styles and descriptions.
3. Pick styles for both the Find What and Replace With criteria, then proceed as described on pages 93–94.

techno note

Up searches back toward the beginning of the document, while Down searches toward the end. All searches the entire document, as you would expect.

Repagination

To display and print page breaks properly, Word must recalculate page endings after you've made changes. Normally Word does this automatically in the background whenever it can steal some otherwise unused computer time. Word always repaginates when:

- You ask it to print
- You are in Print Preview or Page Layout view
- You compile a Table of Contents or Index

To turn off automatic repagination and speed up slower computers when working on large documents:

1. Choose Tools ➤ Options.
2. Click on the General tab if it's not already in view.

3. Uncheck the Background Repagination check box. (You won't be able to do this if you are in Page Layout view.)
4. Close the Options dialog box.
5. Word will repaginate only when you are in a view that requires it. To force repagination, switch to Page Layout, Print Preview, or issue a Print request.

Save, Save As, and Save All

To save files, use standard Windows Save techniques:

- The first time you save a document, selecting File ➤ Save (or clicking the Save button on the Standard toolbar) will open the Save As dialog box. Enter a name for the file and click OK.
- To choose Save options, click the Options button to open the Options dialog box with the Save tab foremost.
- When you save a document you've named, the Save As dialog box won't appear.
- To save a file under a different name, select File ➤ Save As and enter the new name in the Save As dialog box.
- To save changes in all open documents, macros, and templates, select File ➤ Save All. Word will prompt you to save each in turn.

shortcut

Press Ctrl+S to save your document.

Sections

Sections let you change major formatting features at places you decide in your document. You must start a new section whenever you need to:

- Change page orientation within a document
- Change margins in part of a document
- Turn line numbering on or off
- Change footnote appearance or suppress notes
- Change the appearance of headers and footers
- Change the format, position, or progression of page numbers

Inserting Sections

While the exact sequence of events will vary with your project and needs, in general you will:

1. Place the insertion point where you want a new section to begin.
2. Use Insert ➤ Break to create the new section.
3. Make the desired formatting and other changes for that section.
4. Perhaps create other sections farther down in the document.

Sections and the Layout Tab in Page Setup

The options listed in the Section Start drop-down menu on the Layout tab of the Page Setup dialog box (File ➤ Page Setup) are the same as those in the Break dialog box (reached by choosing Insert ➤ Break). This is where you tell Word where you want it to start printing the various sections of your document. You can make a different choice for each section. Here are explanations of your options.

Continuous	(The default setting.) The designated section will start on the page on which the preceding section ends.
New Column	In multicolumn formats, Word breaks a column when it encounters a section mark and prints the subsequent text at the top of a new column.
New Page	Word starts new sections on new pages.
Even Page	Word starts printing the new section on an even-numbered page, even if it means leaving an odd numbered page blank.
Odd Page	Word will start the new section on an odd-numbered page. This is a great way to ensure that new sections start on right-hand pages when designing documents for two-sided printing.

Apply To

The Apply To portion of the Layout tab lets you tell Word how far to go with your requested changes.

This Section	Changes affect only the section containing the insertion point.
This Point Forward	Changes affect the document from the insertion point to the end.
Whole Document	Changes are document-wide.

Copying Section Breaks

Section-formatting information is stored with section breaks. You can copy section information by copying and pasting section breaks. Section breaks differ from paragraph marks (¶), in that a section break controls the information below it, while a paragraph mark controls the information that precedes it. Click on a break to select it.

Deleting Section Breaks

Select a section break as just described. Then press the Backspace or Delete key. Text after the removed section break will take on the characteristics of the preceding material.

Selecting

Word has many ways to select text and other document elements. For instance, you can drag your mouse pointer over the text while holding down the primary mouse button. There are shortcuts for selecting individual words, lines, sentences, and paragraphs.

note

Many of the selection methods involve the *selection bar*, an invisible strip running down the extreme left edge of the document window. When you move the mouse pointer into the selection bar, it turns into an outlined arrow pointing north-north-east.

Selecting Entire Words

Double-click anywhere on a word to select the entire word and the space that follows it. To select adjacent words, drag after double-clicking on the first word.

Selecting Entire Lines

Click once in the selection bar to select the entire line to the right of the mouse pointer.

Selecting Entire Sentences

Hold down Ctrl while you click anywhere in the sentence. This also selects the sentence's punctuation mark and the space following the sentence, if there is one. Dragging after you click this way selects additional sentences.

Selecting Entire Paragraphs

Triple-click anywhere in a paragraph to select it, or double-click in the selection bar to select the adjacent paragraph.

Selecting Your Entire Document

Hold down Ctrl and click in the selection bar to select the whole document. Alternatively, triple-click in the selection bar.

Selecting Graphics and Other Objects

Click anywhere within the graphic or other object. You'll see a border—usually with *handles* (small black boxes) surrounding the selected object.

Shift-Clicking to Select Large Areas

1. Point to the place where you want selection to begin.
2. Click to place the insertion point there.
3. Point to the end of the desired area (scroll if necessary) and hold down the Shift key while you click.

Selecting Rectangular Areas

To select rectangular areas (like columns in a tabbed list), hold down Alt while you drag the mouse.

Spelling Checker

Start the Spelling checker by pressing F7 or by picking Tools ➢ Spelling. The Spelling dialog box appears. Unless you've selected only a portion of your document to check, Word scans down, beginning at the insertion point, and will ask if you want to go back to the top of the document to continue checking, if necessary.

The Spelling checker looks for words that it cannot find in its open dictionaries. When it spots a word that it can't match, Word highlights the questionable characters, scrolls the document so that you can see the problem word in context, and offers you a number of choices.

Typing Your Own Changes

If you want to change a misspelled word only once:

1. Type a replacement in the highlighted Change To box.
2. Press ↵ or click the Change button. Word will replace the problem text with the new text you have typed in the Change To box and then continue spell checking.

To change the word throughout the document that you are checking, click Change All instead of pressing ↵ or clicking Change. If the new word you've typed is something you want Word to recognize in all of your documents, add it to Custom or User Dictionaries.

If you have suggestions enabled, Word will usually list one or more possible spellings.

If you agree with Word's best guess, simply click the Change button to change this occurrence or use the Change All button to change this and all succeeding occurrences of the word. The Spelling Checker will replace the word and continue examining your document.

When it has no suggestions, Word moves the problem text to the Change To box where you can edit it yourself (place a space between two run-together words, for instance).

Using Custom or User Dictionaries

You can maintain as many of your own *custom* dictionaries as you want. Word checks only open dictionaries. The more dictionaries you have open, the slower spell checking will be.

The Standard Custom Dictionary

When you install Word, the installation program places an empty Custom Dictionary in your WINDOWS\MSAPPS\PROOF directory. with the filename CUSTOM.DIC. CUSTOM.DIC is opened and used whenever you spell check unless you instruct Word otherwise. This is where you will want to keep most proper nouns, trademark names, etc.

Word will place words in the Custom Dictionary whenever you click the Add button while spell checking.

Creating a Custom Dictionary

To create a custom dictionary:

1. Select Tools ➤ Options and make sure the Spelling tab is foremost in the Options dialog box.
2. Under Custom Dictionaries, choose the New button.
3. Type a name for the dictionary, then click OK. The new dictionary will thereafter be listed with CUSTOM.DIC in the Spelling dialog box.

techno note

If you add a word to a dictionary as all lowercase, it will be recognized later when it appears in all lowercase, all uppercase, or with an initial capital letter. If you enter a word with only the first letter capitalized, Word will recognize the word when it later appears in all caps or with an initial capital letter, but will question the word if it is all lowercase. Unusual capitalizations like *VisiCalc* will be questioned unless they are stored in the dictionary.

Styles and the Style Gallery

Styles are collections of paragraph and character formatting decisions that make it easy for you to reuse complex paragraph formats without laboriously recreating them each time. Built-in styles are available in all Word documents, and each document can have its own collection of custom styles.

Applying Styles from the Formatting Toolbar

Here are the general steps for applying Word's built-in styles to paragraphs:

1. Either place the insertion point in a paragraph or select several paragraphs.
2. Scroll through the drop-down style list on the Formatting toolbar to pick the desired style. The available items in the list will vary from document to document for reasons you'll soon understand.
3. Click on a style name to apply it to the selected text.
4. Use Edit ➤ Undo if you don't like the results.

Applying Styles from the Keyboard

A few of the commonly used styles have their own keyboard shortcuts. To use them, select text or place the insertion point in the paragraph to be stylized and use one of the following key combinations:

Style	Press
Normal	Ctrl+Shift+N
Heading 1	Alt+Ctrl+1

Style	Press
Heading 2	Alt+Ctrl+2
Heading 3	Alt+Ctrl+3
List Bullet	Ctrl+Shift+L
Style Shown in Toolbar	Ctl+Shift+S

tip

The Edit ➤ Repeat keyboard shortcut (Ctrl+Y) works when applying styles. After you apply a style once, you can move the insertion point to other paragraphs and press Ctrl+Y to apply the new style where needed.

Defining Your Own Styles from the Formatting Toolbar

1. Display the Formatting toolbar if it is not already in view.
2. Place the insertion point in the formatted paragraph whose style you'd like to capture. Make any last-minute changes in style.
3. Click *once* on the style box (the name portion of the drop-down style-name list). The style box will be highlighted, indicating that you can type a new style name.
4. Type a meaningful style name and press ↵.

Word will save the style information and add the new name to the drop-down style list for the current document.

note

Style names can be up to 253 characters long, but shorter is often better. Names can contain any legal characters except backslashes (\), braces ({}), or semicolons (;). Word cares about capitalization in style names.

Using the Style Dialog Box

The Style dialog box lets you define new styles and rename, explore, list, or delete existing ones.

Defining Styles in the Style Dialog Box

1. Place the insertion point in or select a paragraph containing the desired format.
2. Open the Style dialog box (Format ➤ Style).
3. Click on the New button.
4. Type a legal style name in the box provided.
5. Click on OK to record the style.

Defining Keyboard Shortcuts for Styles

To assign keyboard shortcuts, visit the Modify Style Dialog box (reached with the Modify button in the Style dialog box), or use the Keyboard tab of the Customize dialog box (Tools ➤ Customize). For more information, see *To Change Keyboard Shortcuts* on page 20.

Basing One Style Upon Another

Word lets you build upon styles, or base one upon another. Word watches as you develop new styles and bases new styles on the styles you modify.

1. Choose Format ➤ Style.
2. Select the style you plan to base on another.
3. Click the Modify button.
4. When you see the Modify Style dialog box, choose a base style from the Based On list.
5. Make any other necessary changes in the Modify Style dialog box.
6. Click OK when you're done.

tip

To add a style you've created to the template upon which the document you are working on is based, check the Add to Template option in the Modify Style dialog box.

Setting the Next Style

The Modify Style dialog box lets you specify which style Word will flip to when you finish typing a paragraph and press ↵.

1. Choose Format ➤ Style to open the Style dialog box.
2. Select the style you plan to modify.
3. Click the Modify button.
4. In the Modify Style dialog box, choose a "next" style from the Style for Following Paragraph list.
5. Make any other necessary changes in the Modify Style dialog box.
6. Click OK when done.

Printing Out a Style List

1. Open the document of interest.
2. Choose File ➤ Print or press Ctrl+P.
3. Choose Styles from the drop-down Print What list.
4. Click OK.

Using the Style Gallery

By clicking the Style Samples button in the Style Gallery, you can see examples of all of the styles for a document or template. If you are currently working on a project, you can also see how the project would look if you applied styles from various templates.

1. Open a Word project you think you might want to reformat.
2. Open the Gallery with Format ➤ Style Gallery .
3. Click the Style Samples button.
4. Pick a template from the Template list. Wait a moment while Word displays the samples.
5. Choose different template names if you wish to see samples of other style collections.
6. Click the Document button if you want to see the styles automatically applied to the current document.
7. Click OK to close the gallery and apply the new styles or Cancel to close the gallery without changing your document.

Using Reveal Formats or the Style "Cartoon"

To see what formatting a paragraph contains:

1. Click once on the Standard toolbar's Help button. The mouse pointer will grow a big question mark.
2. Point to a paragraph of interest and read about formatting.

Displaying Format Names On-Screen

1. Switch to Normal or Outline view.
2. Choose Tools ➢ Options.
3. Visit the View tab.
4. Pick a style area width (1", perhaps) from the Style Area width section of the View tab.
5. Click OK. Style names will appear at the left of the screen in Normal and Outline views. To remove them, repeat steps 1 through 5 and choose 0 (zero) for the Style Area Width.

When and Where Styles Are Saved

Document and template styles are saved when you save your documents or update your templates. This is yet another good reason to get in the habit of saving early and often.

Word's Standard Styles

Word's designers have created hundreds of standard styles that are used by its footnote, outline, index, table-of-contents, page-numbering, header, and footer features.

Many of the templates for letters, brochures, newsletters, and other documents have their own predefined styles.

Styles that Word Applies Automatically

Word applies these styles automatically:

Style	When Word Applies It
Annotation Text	Comments inserted by the Annotation command
Annotation Reference	Initials of person who inserted the comment
Caption	Captions and table and figure titles
Footer	In footers
Footnote Text	Text in a footnote or endnote
Endnote Text	Footnotes
Footnote Reference	Numbers and characters used as reference marks
Endnote Reference	Reference marks
Header	Header info
Index l–Index 9	Index entries created with Insert ➤ Index and Tables
Line Number	Automatic line numbers
Macro Text	Text of a WordBasic macro
Page Number	Automatic page numbers
TOC 1–TOC 9, Table of Contents	TOC entries
Table of Figures	Automatic figure numbering

Reapplying/Redefining Styles

If you ask Word to apply a style to a paragraph that already uses that style (applying Normal to an already Normal paragraph, for instance), you will be visited by the Replace or Redefine dialog box which serves two purposes. First, it lets you reapply a style to a paragraph that you have inadvertently changed. Second, it lets you quickly redefine a style based on the selected text.

Deleting Styles

1. Open the Style dialog box with Format ➤ Style.
2. Click on the style you want to delete in the Styles list.
3. Click Delete.
4. Click OK to confirm the deletion.
5. The style will be deleted from the current document.

warning

You cannot delete Word's built-in styles.

Renaming Styles

1. Open the Style dialog box with Format ➤ Style.
2. Click on the style you want to rename in the Styles list.
3. Click the Modify button. You will see the Modify Style dialog box.
4. Edit the name in the Name box.

5. Make any other desired changes while in the Modify Style dialog box.
6. Click OK.

reminder

Word cares about capitalization when you name styles. The names *Salutation* and *salutation* are not the same.

Finding and Replacing Styles

You can easily search for and replace styles using Edit ➤ Find and Edit ➤ Replace. In the Find What area of the Find or Replace dialog box, choose the Format button and select Styles from the drop-down list. In the Find Style dialog box, specify the style to find and click OK. Repeat the procedure for the Replace With box if you're replacing.

Transferring Styles between Documents

Select some text from the source document containing the style of interest and paste it into the destination document needing the style. Word will bring over the style with the text.

warning

Remember that if the destination document has a style name identical to the style being copied from the source, the destination document will reformat the incoming text rather than take on the new style. Moreover, if you copy more than fifty styles at once, the source document's entire style sheet will be automatically copied to the destination document.

You can also merge different style sheets, which copies unique styles from a *source* document to a *destination* document and modifies styles with identical names. Here's how:

1. With styles properly named and saved, work in the destination document.
2. Open the Style dialog box with Format ➤ Style.
3. Click on the Organizer button to open the Organizer dialog box with the Styles tab foremost.
4. The name of the source file should appear in the In list at the left side of the dialog box, and probably the file NORMAL.DOT will be specified as the destination or To file on the right of the dialog box.
    - To make the style or styles you are copying globally available, leave the To setting as NORMAL.DOT.
    - To add the style(s) to just a selected document or template, click the *right* Close File button (note that there are two). It will change to an Open File button. Choose the desired destination file using standard Windows file-opening techniques.
5. Pick the styles you wish to copy in the left-hand scrolling list. Click to choose a single style; Shift-click to select ranges; or Ctrl-click to select non-contiguous styles.
6. Click the Copy button.
7. Use the Delete or Rename keys as necessary.
8. Open other source or destination files as necessary, then click Close when you're done.

Symbols and Special Characters

To enter special characters like © and ® or special symbols like ¶, use Insert ➤ Symbol. In the Symbol dialog box, choose the Symbols tab or the Special Characters tab. If you're looking at the Symbols tab and can't find what you want, drop down the Font list and choose a different font. Double click on the desired character to insert it in your text. Click Close when you're finished inserting symbols.

Table of Contents

See *Indexing and Tables of Contents* on page 49.

Tables

Word tables consist of horizontal *rows* and vertical *columns*. You do the typing in areas called *cells*. Cells can contain text, numbers, or graphics. You can edit and embellish text in cells as usual with Word's Formatting toolbar and ruler.

A number of table-specific features let you control the size, shape, and appearance of cells. Border and shading features are available. It is also easy to insert and delete rows and columns.

You can create tables from existing text without needless retyping, or you can use the table feature to organize information and then convert your table to text. You can even import and export spreadsheet data.

The dotted lines around each cell represent *non-printing table gridlines*. You can add printing borders with Format ➤ Borders and Shading. The larger dots are end-of-cell and end-of-row marks. Click the Show ¶ button in the Standard toolbar to reveal them.

Creating a Simple Table

1. Place the insertion point where you want to insert a table (ideally, *not* at the very beginning of an empty document).
2. With the Standard toolbar in view, click the Table button, then drag while holding down the mouse button to highlight the desired number of rows and columns.
3. When the displayed grid represents the desired number of rows and columns, release the mouse button. Word will insert an empty table.

Using the Table Menu to Create a Table

1. Position the insertion point where you want the table (ideally, not at the very beginning of a new, otherwise empty document).
2. Choose Table ➤ Insert Table to open the Table dialog box.
3. Enter the desired number of columns and rows for your table, then click OK.

techno note

Unless you specify a column width in the Column Width box, Word computes a column width automatically, taking into consideration the available text area in your document and the number of columns you've specified. Initially, all table columns are the same width. You can change column widths (see *Changing Column Widths* on page 121).

Entering and Editing Text in a Table

With only a few exceptions, you navigate, enter, and edit table text just as you do any other Word text:

- Use your mouse or arrow keys to position the insertion point, then type normally.
- Think of the cell borders as margins. Word will automatically wrap text within the cell as you reach the right edge. Rows will automatically grow deeper as necessary to accommodate your typing.
- To move from cell to cell within a table, either use your mouse or use the Tab key to go forward and Shift+Tab to go backward.

Selecting in Tables

Select characters, words, and other items in table cells using Word's usual mouse and keyboard features. Moreover, the area between the first character in a cell and the left edge of the cell is called the *cell selection bar*. Clicking on it selects the contents of the entire cell. You can also select an entire cell by dragging with the mouse. Be sure to include the end-of-cell mark in your selection.

To select	Do this
a column	click in the *column selection bar*, the area at the top of a column. (The mouse pointer changes into a large, down-pointing arrow when it's over the column selection bar.) Alternatively, hold down the Alt key and click anywhere in a column.

To select	Do this
a column	Selecting the bottom or top cell in a column and dragging up or down is somewhat tedious, but will also work.
a row	Double-click any cell selection bar, or select the leftmost or rightmost cell in a row and drag.
groups of adjacent cells	either drag through the cells or click in one cell and Shift-click in the others.
the whole table	hold down Alt and double-click anywhere in the table. If your document contains multiple tables and they are not separated by paragraph marks, this technique will select all adjacent tables.

warning

Do *not* use Edit ➤ Select All to select a table—that will select the whole document instead. Use Table ➤ Select Table.

Adding Table Borders that Print

Select the cell or cells you wish to surround, then use the line thickness portion of the Borders toolbar. Pick the desired combination of line thicknesses and apply the borders just as you would add them to paragraphs.

Adding Rows at the End of a Table

To add a new row at the end of an existing table, place the insertion point anywhere in the last cell (the one in the lower-right corner of your table) and press the Tab key. Word will insert a new row using the styles of the cells immediately above.

Adding Rows in the Middle of a Table

1. Place the insertion point in the row above which you want the new row.
    - To add multiple rows, select as many existing rows as you want to insert new ones—for example, to add three rows, select the three existing rows beneath the desired insertion point.
2. Select Table ➤ Insert Rows.

Changing Row Heights

Normally, Word sets the height of each row automatically to accommodate the cell containing the tallest entry. For instance, if one cell in a row needs 2.0" to accommodate the text or graphic it contains, all of the cells in that row will be 2.0" high. All cells in a row must be the same height, but different rows can have different heights.

To change row height manually:

1. Click anywhere in the row you wish to resize.
2. Move the pointer to the vertical ruler at the left edge of the screen watching the pointer as you move it.
3. When it becomes an up-and-down arrow, use it to drag the row to the desired height.
4. Release the mouse button.

Resizing Rows with Table ➢ Cell Height and Width

Overrule Word's automatic row-height (and column-width) settings via Table ➢ Cell Height and Width:

1. Place the insertion point anywhere in the row whose height you wish to specify. If you want multiple rows to share the same height, select all of them.
2. Choose Table ➢ Cell Height and Width.
3. Click on the Row tab if necessary to reveal its choices.
4. Use the Height drop-down list to choose At Least or Exactly.
5. Enter the desired dimension in points, inches, centimeters, and so on. (The default is points).
6. To change settings for previous or next rows, click the Previous or Next buttons.
7. Click OK to make the change and close the dialog box.

If the exact height you specify is too small to accommodate the biggest entry in a row, the excessive text or a portion of the too-tall graphic will be cropped when printed. Simply increase the row height if this is undesirable.

Deleting Rows

Select the row or rows to be deleted, then use Table ➢ Delete Rows. This will delete both the rows themselves (the cells) and their contents (text or graphics or whatever) To delete the *contents* of cells but leave the cells intact, select text or graphics and press Delete.

Changing the Spacing between Rows

To change the amount of white space between rows, select the paragraph of interest, choose Format ➤ Paragraph and specify the Before and After spacing of the first or last paragraphs in the cells.

Inserting Columns in the Middle of a Table

1. Select the column to the *right* of where you want the new column to appear.
2. Click the Table button in the Standard toolbar (notice how its name has changed to Insert Columns) or choose Table ➤ Insert Columns.
3. Word will add a new column but will not change the width of the earlier columns to accommodate it. To make the enlarged table fit on your page, you will probably need to adjust margins, column widths, or change page orientation. New columns retain the format of the old rightmost columns, but borders will not transfer.

tip

To insert multiple columns, select as many existing columns as you want to insert new ones to the right of the desired location of the new columns.

Inserting Columns at the Right Edge of a Table

1. Select an end-of-row marker.
2. Click on the Table button in the Standard toolbar (notice how its name has changed to Insert Cells):
3. In the Insert Cells dialog box, pick Insert Entire Column.
4. Click OK.

Deleting Columns

1. Select the column or columns to be removed. The choices on the Table menu change to include column-related commands.
2. Choose Table ➤ Delete Columns.

Changing Column Widths

You can change the widths of entire columns or of selected cells within columns. Most changes can be made by dragging column markers on the table scale in the ruler. But you can make precision adjustments in the Cell Height and Width dialog box.

1. Point to a column boundary. The pointer will change shape.
2. Drag the column width marker. Watch the dotted line and ruler settings, and release the moue button when the column is the desired width.

If you hold down Shift while dragging, the column to the right changes size while the table's overall width remains unchanged. (Note that this affects two columns: the one being dragged and one whose width is encroached upon.)

If you hold down Ctrl while dragging, all columns to the right change size, but the table's overall width does not.

You can also drag the column markers on the ruler to change column widths. Just don't accidentally drag the cells' indent markers instead.

note

You can also change the width of one or more cells by selecting them and visiting the Cell Height and Width dialog box (Table ➤ Cell Height and Width). Specify a new width on the Columns tab.

Changing Table Cell Widths with the AutoFit Button

1. Select the cells you wish to resize, or more often the entire table.
2. Choose Table ➤ Cell Height and Width.
3. Reveal the Column tab if it is not already in view.
4. Click on the AutoFit button. Word will snug-up the selected cells.

Merging Cells

Use the Merge Cells feature to combine the contents of multiple cells—for example, to make a heading in one cell span an entire table or selected group of columns. Select the cells to merge, then choose Table ➤ Merge Cells, and the contents of the designated cells will merge. You may need to reformat text merged this way.

Unmerging Cells

1. Place the insertion point in a merged cell.
2. Choose Table ➤ Split Cells. You'll be asked how many cells you want after the split.

Changing the Space between Columns

Word assigns cell widths based on the available text area and the number of columns you request. In the process, it sets aside a small amount of unprintable space between (actually within) each cell.

To change the space between columns:

1. Select the columns of interest
2. Select Table ➤ Cell Height and Width to visit the Columns tab of the Cell Height and Width dialog box.
3. Type a new specification in the Space Between Columns box, or use the arrows to flip through suggested choices.
4. Click OK.

AutoFormatting Tables

Table ➤ Table AutoFormat attempts to pick cell settings that make a presentable table.

1. Enter, edit, spell-check, reorganize and otherwise finish with your table.
2. Save your document to disk.
3. Select the entire table (Alt+5 on the numeric keypad with Num Lock off).

4. Choose Table ➤ Table AutoFormat.
5. Preview the format choices from the scrolling list by highlighting their names one at a time. ↑ and ↓ are handy here. Pay particular attention to how Word handles row and column headings in the preview examples.
6. Pick a style by highlighting it and click OK.

Converting Text to Tables

Highlight the text that you want to turn into a table. Choose Table ➤ Convert Text to Table and click the appropriate option button (text divided by paragraphs, tabs, or commas) in the resulting dialog box.

Converting Tables to Text

Select the table cells you wish to convert, hold down Alt and double-click to select the whole table. Choose Table ➤ Convert Table to Text. Word will display a Table to Text dialog box, which asks if you want the table converted to paragraphs, tab-delimited text, or comma-delimited text. Pick one. If you pick the comma or tab options, Word will convert each row of your table into one line (a paragraph, actually). Cells in your old tables will become tab- or comma-separated items on the lines.

note

Choosing the paragraph option will convert each old table cell into at least one paragraph. If cells contain multiple paragraphs, the paragraph marks are retained during the conversion, so some cells will create more than one new paragraph.

Using the Table Wizard

You can also produce tables using the Table Wizard. The Wizard will ask you some questions and format your table.

1. Place the insertion point where you want the table. Tap ↵ once or twice if you've just opened a new document.
2. Choose Table ➤ Insert Table.
3. Click the Wizard button in the Table dialog box. You will be presented with a number of screens asking you questions.
4. Look at each choice *carefully*, and study the examples if they are given. Don't confuse *rows* and *columns* when the Wizard gives you choices. Try to imagine *your* data in the sample table formats.
5. Click on the Next button after each choice or Back to back up one screen.
6. When the Wiz runs out of questions, click Finish. You'll be presented with the Table AutoFormat dialog box (which you read about earlier).
7. Cruise the format samples until you find just the right mood. Click OK, and see what develops.

Tabs

Each paragraph in a Word document can have the same or different tab settings. Word offers five specialized tab stop types. They each work with tabs to help align text, and are particularly useful for making simple columnar lists.

- *Left* tab stops are like the plain vanilla ones you find on your old Smith Corona. Text typed at these tab stops bumps up against the left edge of the stop.

- Center tab stop center your text around the tab stops.
- Right tab stops position whatever you type to the left of the tab.This is a great way to type long lists of numbers and have them line up.
- Decimal tab stops behave as you'd expect. They align columns of numbers on the decimal point and are perfect for simple financial reports.
- The Bar button creates nice, thin vertical lines that separate columns. They aren't actual tab stops (you can't use them to align text) but you can place and move them like stops.

Setting Custom Tab Stops

You can create custom tabs locations to replace Word's defaults. Tab stops are always stored with the paragraph mark for each paragraph, thus all of the rules about paragraph marks apply (see page 38 for more information). You can set custom tabs as you type or use the standard tabs initially and then go back to fine-tune them.

1. With the ruler in view, click the button at the left edge of the horizontal ruler repeatedly until it shows the icon for the desired tab stop type (Left, Center, Right, or Decimal).
2. Click on the ruler where you want to place a tab stop. If you make a mistake, drag the stop off the ruler and try again.
3. When you type, press Tab to move the insertion point to the new tab positions. With Show ¶ turned on, you'll see fat arrows indicating each tab character you type.

Moving Tab Stops on the Ruler

Simply point to a stop of interest and drag it. If you have already entered text that uses the tab stops you want to move, first select all of the text before moving the tab stop.

Setting Tab Stops with the Tabs Dialog Box

Produce the Tabs dialog box using one of these methods:

- Double-click any tab stop on the ruler.
- Choose Format ➤ Tabs.
- Click the Tabs button in the Paragraph dialog box.
- Double-click in the lower half of the ruler to place a new left tab stop where you have clicked *and* bring up the Tabs dialog box. The position of the new tab stop will be shown in the Tab Stop Position area of the dialog box and will change as you move the tab stop.

In the Tabs dialog box, enter a position in the Tab Stop Position box, select an Alignment, specify a Leader if you want one (see the next section), and click the Set button. Repeat until satisfied, then click the OK button.

note

Double-clicking the upper half of the ruler will bring up the Page Setup dialog box.

Using Leader Characters for Tabs

Here's how to set tab leader characters such as dots, hyphens, or underscores:

1. Select the paragraphs you want to pretty-up.
2. Click on the tab where you want the leaders.
3. Choose a leader style from the Tabs dialog box.
4. Click OK.

tip

You can apply tab leaders when defining new tab stops or by double-clicking on existing stops to bring up the Tabs dialog box as an afterthought.

Clearing Tab Stops

To clear tab stops, open the Tabs dialog box (Format ➤ Tabs):

- To clear one tab, highlight it in the Tab Stop Position box and click the Clear button.
- To clear all tabs, click the Clear All button.

shortcut

You can drag the occasional tab off the ruler if you don't need it.

Templates, Wizards, and Sample Documents

Templates are read-only documents containing styles and other design elements that you can use to create or restyle your own documents. *Wizards* are like computerized assistants. Like you, Wizards also use templates to create documents, after asking some questions and making a few design decisions on their own. *Sample documents* are examples created by Microsoft to show you what can be done. They are great learning tools.

These are the template, Wizard, and sample documents supplied with Word:

Templates (.DOT)	Wizards (.WIZ)	Sample Documents (.DOC)
BROCHUR1	AGENDA	CLASSIC1
DIRECTR1	AWARD	CLASSIC2
FAXCOVR1	CALENDAR	CLASSIC3
FAXCOVR2	CV	CLASSIC4
INVOICE	FAX	JAZZY1
LETTER1	LEGAL	JAZZY2
LETTER2	LETTER	JAZZY3
LETTER3	MEMO	JAZZY4
MANUAL1	NEWSLTTR	MODERN1
MANUSCR1	RESUME	MODERN2
MANUSCR3	TABLE	MODERN3
MEMO1	—	MODERN4
MEMO2	—	MEMO3.DOT
NORMAL	—	—
PRESENT1	—	—
PRESREL1	—	—
PRESREL2	—	—

Templates (.DOT)	Wizards (.WIZ)	Sample Documents (.DOC)
PRESREL3	—	—
PURCHORD	—	—
REPORT1	—	—
REPORT2	—	—
REPORT3	—	—
RESUME1	—	—
RESUME2	—	—
RESUME4	—	—
THESIS1	—	—
WEEKTIME	—	—

If you did a complete installation, these files will all be located in their own subdirectory called TEMPLATE. Look for the TEMPLATE subdirectory in your Word directory.

There are at least four different ways to use templates:

- Start new projects based on templates shipped with Word.
- Modify existing projects by choosing templates and *completely reformat* your work in the template's styles.
- Copy *selected* styles from templates for use in your projects.
- Create and save new templates of your own creation.

Template Types

Word's standard templates come in up to four different "flavors." Microsoft refers to these as *Template Types*:

- Classic (type 1)
- Contemporary (type 2)
- Typewriter (type 3)
- Elegant (type 4)

The different types give documents different "moods." For instance, a Classic Letter template uses Times Roman, while a Contemporary letter uses Arial. The Company Name style in the Contemporary letter template includes a border, while the Classic type does not, and so on. Not all templates come in all types. For instance, there is only one Elegant document titled RESUME4.DOT. Here's a summary of the rest:

Template type	**Classic (.DOT)**	**Contemporary (.DOT)**	**Typewriter (.DOT)**
Brochure	BROCHURl	—	—
Directory	DIRECTRl	—	—
Fax cover sheet	FAXCOVR1	FAXCOVR2	—
Letter	LETTER1	LETTER2	LETTER3
Manual	MANUALl	—	—
Manuscript	MANUSCR1	—	MANUSCR3
Memo	MEM01	MEM02	MEM03
Normal	NORMAL.DOC	—	—
Presentation	PRESENTl	—	—
Press release	PRESREL1	PRESREL2	PRESREL3
Purchase order	PURCHORD	—	—
Report	REPORTI	REPORT2	REPORT3
Resume	RESUMEl	RESUME2	—
Thesis	THESIS1	—	—
Timesheet	WEEKTIME	—	—

Modifying Templates

You can change templates just as you would any other Word documents. The only difference is one additional step you must take when saving your work.

1. Use File ➤ Open to open the template.
2. Make the changes, such as adding your logo and other embellishments.
3. Print out a sample and check your work.
4. When you are satisfied, choose File ➤ Save As.
5. Type the exact same filename as the old template if you want to replace the old template, or type a new filename if you want to keep *both* the old and new (make sure to type the extension .DOT if you choose a new file name).

Toolbars

See the inside front cover, *Options* (page 66), *Customizing Word* (page 18), and on-line help to learn about toolbars.

Views

Word can show you your document with varying levels of detail to make things easier to visualize or quicker to work with. Word provides five different views:

- Normal view
- Page Layout view
- Outline view
- Print Preview
- Split screen

Using Normal View

Use Normal view for most of your heavy-duty text entry and editing. Word's other views respond noticeably slower to typing, editing, and scrolling.

Normal view keeps repagination and screen redraw delays to a minimum. It shows your text as you have typed it, and displays graphics where you've inserted them (which is not necessarily where they'll print).

Normal view does not show side-by-side column positioning, footers, headers, nor the printing position of framed items. Columns are shown at their actual width, but not side-by-side. Automatic page breaks are shown as dotted lines. Manual page breaks, if you've defined any, are shown as darker lines containing the words *Page Break*, while section breaks are double dark lines with the words *End of Section*, and so on. Line numbers will not appear in Normal view.

You can create and edit text, columns, and graphics as usual in Normal view. To work on headers or footers, select View ➤ Header and Footer; Word will automatically switch you to Page Layout view.

Switching Views

To switch views, pull down the View menu and select Normal, Outline, or Page Layout views, or use the three buttons in the bottom-left corner of Word's status area (from left to right: Normal view, Page Layout View, and Outline View).

note

To switch to Print Preview, select File ➤ Print Preview; press Ctrl+Alt+I; or press Ctrl+F2.

Page Layout View

In Page Layout view, the screen resembles a white sheet of paper, or at least a portion of a sheet. You will see a dark background that Word places behind the "paper." On a large enough screen, you will see the whole page. On smaller screens, or when using a large paper setting in Page Setup, you may need to scroll to see these representations of the paper's edges.

Editing in Page Layout View

Generally, you edit as usual in Page Layout view. Text and graphics are positioned where they will print. Headers and footers can be both seen and edited. Click in a header, footer, or body text to position the insertion point. Page breaks, be they automatic or forced, are represented by new pages on the screen rather than by dashed lines in the text. You can scroll from page to page, as you'd expect.

Headers and Footers in Page Layout View

You can see headers and footers in Page Layout view. To edit them, click anywhere in a header or footer. It will "undim," and be surrounded by a dashed line. The Header and Footer toolbar will also appear if it's not already on your screen.

You can format text in headers just as you would anywhere else in a Word document. For instance, to right-align header text, place the insertion point in the text (or select multiple lines in the header and use the Format menu's Right-align button.

reminder

To add date or time entries and page numbering to headers and footers, use the buttons on the Header and Footer toolbar.

Using Split-Screen View

Use the split screen to keep two widely separated portions of a document in view at the same time. To split the screen, point to the small black rectangle in the upper-right corner of your Word document window. The pointer will change to the split-bar pointer; drag this down to divide the screen. When you release the mouse button, your screen will split into two independent windows, each with its own scroll bar.

shortcut

To split the screen in half, double-click the black rectangle.

To return to a single screen, either double-click the split-bar or drag it to the top or bottom of the screen.

shortcut

To return to a single screen, press Alt+Shift+C.

Using Print Preview

Print Preview is more than just another way to view documents. Choose File ➤ Print Preview or use Ctrl+Alt+I or Ctrl+F2.

Using the Zoom Control

Depending on your screen size and settings, you will see either an unreadable bird's-eye view of a page or two, or you will see a full, readable page. Use the Zoom Control drop-down list or the Magnifier button and magnifier pointer to produce a readable size.

Viewing Multiple Pages

Click the One Page to view one page. To view more pages, click the Multiple Pages button and drag the grid until it displays the number of pages you want (up to 3x7).

Repositioning Margins

If the ruler is hidden, display it by clicking the View Ruler button. Drag a margin boundary on the horizontal ruler to change the right or left margin, or a margin boundary on the vertical ruler to change the top or bottom margin.

new in Word 6

You can edit text or headers and footers in Print Preview—a great improvement over previous versions of Word. Click the Magnifier button on the Print Preview toolbar to turn off the Magnifier pointer and produce a normal insertion point, then edit your heart out. Click the Magnifier button again to restore the Magnifier.

shortcut

The button that looks like a magnifying glass and a piece of paper on the Standard toolbar will switch you to Print Preview mode. Use the Close button in Print Preview to bring you back to whatever view you were in previously.

Outline View

See *Outlines* on page 87.

Showing Paragraph Marks, Spaces, Etc.

Word can display helpful non-printing characters to let you see what's going on. Examples include:

- Paragraph marks (¶)
- Dots denoting spaces
- Arrows denoting tab characters
- Dashed lines for page breaks
- Text and graphic boundaries

To toggle the display of these items, use the ¶ button on the Standard toolbar. (It's near the right edge.)

Zooming

The little drop-down list near the right end of the Formatting toolbar is called the Zoom Control. It lets you zoom in and out to see bigger or smaller on-screen representations. It does not affect printing size.

see also

Full Screen (page 42)

INDEX

Boldface page numbers indicate definitions and principal discussions of primary topics and subtopics.

Symbols

A

B

G

H

I

J

K

L

P

Q

R

S

T

U

V

W

Z

Mail Merge Toolbar

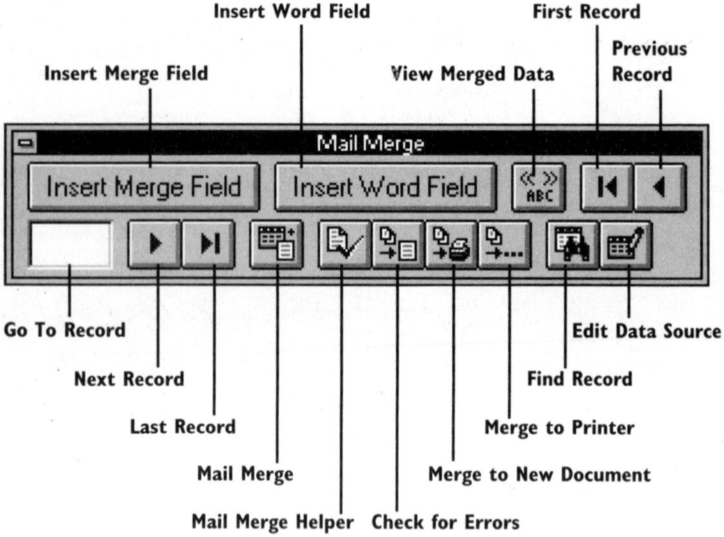

Macro Toolbar

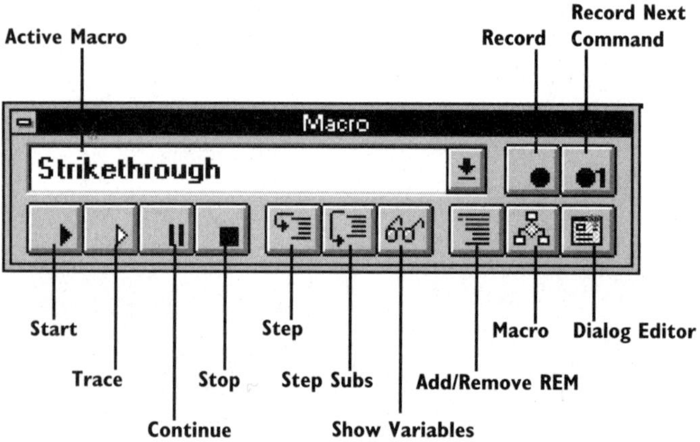